Public Relations: A Managem

A Penning Ink Publication

Penning Ink
15636 River Side Drive
Spring Lake, MI 49456
www.penningink.com

ISBN: 978-0-9890956-6-2 (e-book)
          978-0-9890956-7-9 (paperback)

Part I: Foundations   3

CHAPTER 1: PUBLIC RELATIONS AS MANAGEMENT   4

CHAPTER 2: BUSINESS KNOWLEDGE AND PR   14

CHAPTER 3: THE PR PROCESS   22

Part II: Publics   32

CHAPTER 4: EMPLOYEE RELATIONS   33

CHAPTER 5: COMMUNITY RELATIONS   41

CHAPTER 6: GOVERNMENT RELATIONS & PUBLIC AFFAIRS   47

CHAPTER 7: INVESTOR RELATIONS   54

CHAPTER 8: CONSUMER RELATIONS   63

CHAPTER 9: INTERNATIONAL PUBLIC RELATIONS   70

Part III: Special Situations   77

CHAPTER 10: CRISIS COMMUNICATION   78

CHAPTER 11: INTEGRATED COMMUNICATIONS   87

PUBLIC RELATIONS:
A MANAGEMENT FUNCTION

Public relations is a function in many organizations. Like any other function, it needs to be managed to be successful. But that is NOT what this book is about. If so it would have been called "Public Relations Management."

Instead, *Public Relations: A Management Function* makes the point that the work of public relations is part of the management of the entire organization, be it a business, nonprofit or government entity. In other words, savvy public relations professionals should work to help CEOs and others in the "C-suite" to accomplish their broader organizational goals.

The book starts in Part I by laying a foundation for readers to understand business and management concepts, and then offers a review of the basic work of public relations by focusing on its accepted RACE process. Part II, the bulk of the book, offers chapters focused on specific publics with whom organizations seek to have mutually beneficial relationships. Finally, Part III goes beyond publics to address specific situations in public relations practice that are critical to management, including crisis communication and integrated communications.

Dr. Timothy Penning worked as a journalist and a public relations professional before becoming a professor. He teaches public relations courses—including Public Relations Management—at Grand Valley State University in Michigan and continues to provide public relations consulting to various clients. He has a Ph.D. in media and information studies from Michigan State University and is accredited in public relations (APR) by the Public Relations Society of America (PRSA). He is a member of the PRSA College of Fellows and the Arthur W. Page Society.

Part I: Foundations

This section will cover why PR is a management function, fundamental business principles, and review the established process for practice of public relations.

CHAPTER 1: PUBLIC RELATIONS AS MANAGEMENT

In 2012, the Public Relations Society of America (PRSA) decided to update its definition of public relations. It did so by polling members and paring down responses to three final candidates. Then by vote the final version was adopted:

"Public relations is a strategic communication process that builds mutually beneficial relationships between organizations and their publics."

The value of that definition is that it is concise, and also stresses the "strategic" and "relationship" aspect of public relations. It also positions public relations as a profession that brings organizations and their multiple publics together, something known as OPRs—organization-public relationships.

However, in an effort to streamline the definition, one plank from a previous definition was left out—public relations is a "management function."

Some argue that such a concept is implied in the definition above. However, others maintain that it is important to be explicit that *public relations is a management function*. The reason is that too many people outside the profession, as well as many who practice public relations, have a limited understanding of public relations.

Some see it as only publicity and media relations, which is one tactic but only about 10% of what PR people do, and some do none at all. Others may say PR is about "getting the word out" or "raising awareness." Again, there is some value in that but it is limited in scope and amateur in its understanding of the profession. Even those who speak of PR management often only do so to the extent that they consider the public relations function needs to be managed and strategic.

But all of the above misses the point. Public relations is a management function for a simple yet profound reason:

Public relations is a management function because it helps in significant ways to accomplish the management goals of the entire organization.

Those who understand public relations properly, including the definition above, can see how this emphasis on management makes sense. The success of any organization is heavily dependent on the relationship it has with numerous publics, both inside and outside the organization. It is the public relations executive who is naturally concerned with ALL of these publics, where as some other management positions and functions are understandably focused on one or several publics. For example, human resources has a natural focus on employees, and marketing is concerned primarily with customers.

In a sense, public relations is more about organization-public relationships than it is about communication. Communication is how public relations professionals do what they do, but relationships are the essence of what they do. The success of the organization in meeting its mission is the ultimate purpose.

This is why successful public relations professionals can speak the language of the "C-suite." Often, a top PR person at an organization is called a Chief Communication Officer, or CCO. But they can't only focus on communications. They have to be well-versed in the functions and concerns of their colleagues who are 'chiefs' of other areas of the organization, including human resources, finance, operations, marketing, and others, all of which report to the chief of chiefs, the Chief Executive Officer (CEO). If a PR person or CCO can't explain why public relations contributes to all areas of an organization, they don't have a management mindset.

Theoretical and Practical Basis for PR as Management

The assertion that PR is a management function does not come without a solid foundation. There is a rich theoretical background to public relations generally, and specifically there is much evidence that public relations if properly practiced contributes to broader managerial success.

Keep in mind that "theory" does not mean an abstraction or guess at something. True theory is actually the most practical way of looking at things, because theory is based on significant evidence. In the case of public relations in management, there are two main theoretical considerations—the Excellence Theory and the Page Principles.

The Excellence Theory

The Excellence Theory[1] resulted from 15 years of research that included surveys of top public relations executives and observations of the public relations work in numerous organizations. It merged lots of other specific theory ranging from public relations roles to employee communications and more. The Excellence Theory has been repeatedly cited in subsequent academic research and has informed the practice of PR since it first emerged in 1992.

Essentially, the Excellence Theory determined from all its evidence that organizations have "excellent" public relations if:

- PR is a **management role** in organization, meaning the top PR person is part of the 'C-Suite' and reports to the CEO or Executive Director;

- PR is involved in **strategic decision making** affecting the entire organization, not just overseeing employees in the PR or communications department, and not only being called on to communicate decisions after they are made;

- PR is **integrated** with other functions, but not simply as integrated marketing communications (IMC) (There is a chapter on IC vs IMC later in this book). In other words, PR should not just be used to help sell products and services, but to create a productive employee culture, gain voice with government policy makers, and a host of other collaborative roles;

- PR is practiced with the **two-way symmetrical** principle. One of the aspects of the Excellence Theory is the emergence of the four models of PR practice. The most advanced of these is two-way symmetrical, which is characterized by organizations listening to their various publics and working toward mutual understanding and relationships of mutual benefit, not merely one-way communications of two-way asymmetrical communications which only involves listening to ensure the organization's goals are always paramount over the public interest;

---

[1] Grunig, J.E. (2008). *Excellence Theory in Public Relations. In The International Encyclopedia of Communication*, W. Donsbach (Ed.). doi:10.1002/9781405186407.wbiece047

- PR promotes **social responsibility**, or a value to society broadly and not just the organization's self-interest. This was a radical concept in the early 1990s but in recent years the prevalence of sustainability, corporate social responsibility (CSR), ESG (environmental, social, and governance) factors of management, B-corporations, and corporate 'purpose' have made this not a nice distinction but a requirement;

- PR promotes **diversity** of gender, race and more. Again, this was a relatively novel concept when the theory first emerged. But today, diversity and inclusion (D&I) efforts are not only common, but an expectation in organizations. Not only that, but the public expects these efforts to be genuine and transparent.

- PR is the **ethical** counsel of the organization. Note that this doesn't just mean that public relations is practiced in an ethical way. This means the top PR person serves as the ethical counsel for the whole organization, providing ethical advice to the CEO, human resources, marketing and others. More recent research has shown that more PR people, thanks to ethics courses in PR programs in college and ethics training by PR associations, are willing to embrace this role. And, it makes sense because of all organizational functions, PR is the only one concerned with ALL publics, and as noted above the concern is. for mutual relationships and not organizational self interest.

- PR is a **global** function, practiced through the whole organization. This is somewhat the same as the emphasis given in earlier points, but it bears. Singling out as a specific aspect of excellent PR. Essentially, all of the above points must be embraced not just in the PR department, but in all parts of an organization. This is really about **culture**.

From this list, and the theory, it is obvious that Excellent PR is so much more than a set of communication tactics. It is about persuading everyone in a company, nonprofit or other organization to understand and act according to the principles of excellent public relations.

Some would argue that all of this is too "idealistic." That's another way of saying that the Excellence Theory is a "normative" theory, a type of theory that asserts how things ought to be. And that is true in part. But the Excellence Theory is also an "empirical" theory, meaning it has been observed. Specifically, it has been observed in this and other research that organizations that practice public relations in this way actually are more successful at meeting organizational goals in terms of operations, finance, and reputation.

The Page Principles

The Page Principles are named for Arthur Page, a PR professional who practiced in the early to mid 1900s. He is legendary as one of the first to see PR as a management function. Already in 1927, his title was Vice President of Public Relations at AT&T, one of the largest companies in the world at the time. When many "public relations" people were focused on dealing with the news media, Page was one of the first to say he had moved beyond news releases and focused his time counseling management on their relationships with their publics.

Over the years, in speeches and other statements, Page articulated his views of PR as a management function. Others pored over these and determined a set of principles that came from how Page practiced. These are preserved and promoted by a society today that bears his name, the <u>Arthur W. Page Society</u>, a group of CCOs who share his philosophy of practice.

The Page Principles from a theory perspective are more critical (based on reason) or normative (the way things ought to be). They guide PR as a management practice are as follows, directly from the Page Society web site:

1. **Tell the truth**—Let the public know what's happening with honest and good intention; provide an ethically accurate picture of the enterprise's character, values, ideals and actions.

2. **Prove it with action**—Public perception of an enterprise is determined 90 percent by what it does and 10 percent by what it says.

3. **Listen to stakeholders**—To serve the enterprise well, understand what the public wants and needs and advocate for engagement with all stakeholders. Keep top decision makers and other employees informed about stakeholder reaction to the enterprise's products, policies and practices. To listen effectively, engage a diverse range of stakeholders through inclusive dialogue.

4. **Manage for tomorrow**—Anticipate public reaction and eliminate practices that create difficulties. Generate goodwill.

5. **Conduct public relations as if the whole enterprise depends on it**—No strategy should be implemented without considering its impact on stakeholders. As a management and policymaking function, public relations should encourage the enterprise's decision making, policies and actions to consider its stakeholders' diverse range of views, values, experience, expectations and aspirations.

6. **Realize an enterprise's true character is expressed by its people**—The strongest opinions — good or bad — about an enterprise are shaped by the words and deeds of an increasingly diverse workforce. As a result, every employee — active or retired — is involved with public relations. It is the responsibility of corporate communications to advocate for respect, diversity and inclusion in the workforce and to support each employee's capability and desire to be an honest, knowledgeable ambassador to customers, friends, share owners and public officials.

7. **Remain calm, patient and good-humored**—Lay the groundwork for public relations successes with consistent and reasoned attention to information and stakeholders. When a crisis arises, remember, cool heads communicate best.

Whereas the Excellence Theory is based on academic research and surveys of numerous practitioners, the Page Principles are derived from the long and extensive practice of one professional and confirmed subsequently by others. Taken together, they make the case and provide guidance for PR being practiced as a management function. However, PR is not always practiced in this proven effective way. But anyone going into the field should strive to do so.

Influences on the Practice of PR as Management

In a perfect world, everyone would accept the fact that PR is a management function and practice accordingly. But PR practice can be influenced in a way that prevents that, and those influences are at the level of the practitioner, the organization, and the environment beyond the organization.[2]

Individual Influences

With regard to the practitioner or the people who actual do the public relations job, a lot depends on their own training. If they have a college degree in public relations and/or are accredited in public relations (APR) goes a long way to them being equipped to practice PR with the broad perspective described above. Also, if they have experience in the field of public relations at previous jobs before coming to their current organization is a determinant of them practicing with a management orientation.

Finally, much research in public relations "roles" has determined that professionals may "enact" either a technician or manager role. A technician is one concerned primarily with producing tactics, the content of which is often determined by others. A manager role by comparison is everything stressed in this chapter. The key is, a public relations professional has to *choose* to act like a manager and assert themselves in advising others. But some are content to just be glorified writers or communication producers.

Organizational Influences

The organization itself can influence whether PR is practiced as a management level, even if the professional tries to do so. One factor has to do with structure, and where the PR function or department is placed. If PR is under marketing in a company, or development in a nonprofit, its role is inappropriately limited to sales or fundraising, That's why the public relations function should be situated as its own department or unit, with the top professional reporting directly to the CEO.

---

[2] Penning, T. (2011) *Factors Affecting Organizational Blog Content: Public Relations Practitioners and Organizational Context.* Proquest. ISBN 978-1243819727

Similarly, the top PR person should be part of what researchers call the 'dominant coalition'. This informal group of people in an organization can change over time, but essentially these are the people who make the decisions for the organization. The top PR person can more ably act as a manager if they are part of this group and involved in making decisions, not merely communicating them.

Encroachment is another organizational influence on whether or not PR is practiced as a management function. In football, encroachment means a player stepped over the line of scrimmage onto the other team's side. In organizations, encroachment means someone with expertise in one management function "steps over the line" and onto the "turf" of the public relations professional. For example, a marketing manager editing a news release to be more "sales" oriented, an HR director changing a statement to be less transparent, or a lawyer assuming the role of spokesperson in a crisis.

Finally, the model of PR practiced can influence whether PR is a management function. Mere press agentry or public information are simple one-way models. As noted above, two-way symmetrical is more akin to a management perspective of PR that stresses long-term, mutual relationships and not just getting the word out.

Environmental Influences

Whether or not PR is practiced as a management function can also be influenced by the environment beyond the organization. If an organization works in a lot of uncertainty because of the industry it is in or times of economic turmoil, PR may be called upon to be more strategic and assist the CEO in the direction of the company. The same is true if the organization is in a highly competitive environment or one in which there is a lot of government regulation, or the potential for it.

Getting a "Seat at the Table"

PR people often talk about trying to get a "seat at the table." The table in reference is the one the management team sits around for management meetings, or the senior leadership team meeting or whatever it is called in a given organization. The key for a PR professional to practice PR as management is. to be in that meeting and at that table, providing insight and advice as to the what the organization should do. They should not wait for others in that room to make the decisions and then emerge and tell the PR person to communicate them.

One way to get a set at the table is to understand general business principles, and to understand the specific business an organization is in. Or, if non-profit or government office, what is the cause or mission. This will be the subject of chapter 2. But for now it is important to consider the ways a PR professional proves they are worthy to be "at the table."

One way of earning that right is to approach things from a higher level. This means not just proposing ideas and solutions that are creative, but strategic. There are many ways people define "strategy" or "strategic," but the essence of strategy is that is purposeful and tied to fulfilling the organization's mission. If an idea is just clever, but has no clear purpose (or the word that will be used throughout this book is "objective"), it is not strategic. If an idea is really good communication but can not be shown to be relevant to mission, it is not strategic.

In other words, strategic communication has these characteristics:

• It is purposeful, or has a defined intent

• It will accomplish something specific

• It is connected to organizational mission (i.e. management objectives)

• It is NOT just a tactic

A good rule of thumb is to not speak about how great a PR suggestion is in terms of the communication attributes, but how it solves a management concern. For example, to talk about the seamless interface of an overhauled web site is nice from a tactical perspective, but to demonstrate how it will lead to higher employee retention or customer leads is of interest to management.

Some of the more common issues of concern to management include organizational reputation, stakeholder relationships, organizational credibility, and public trust. PR practitioners who speak only of getting awareness will not be considered management material. To be a true PR professional (i.e. not a mere practitioner), one must address these broader concerns and show how communication can be a specific solution.

One way to summarize the concept of PR being a management function is to think of how the relationship between a PR professional and a CEO has evolved over the years. Several veteran professionals and academics have described this evolution as following a progression of three steps:

1. CEOs want to know HOW to say it? (After situations occurred)

2. Then CEOs want to know WHAT to say and WHEN (Strategy)

3. Finally CEOs want to know not just what to say but what to DO? (Part of decision making and management).

PR professionals should seek to work for and with CEOs who have the third perspective. But PR professionals also have to be able to offer what these CEOs. want. The purpose of this book is to provide the ability to do so.

CHAPTER 2: BUSINESS KNOWLEDGE AND PR

Some students—and professionals—in public relations shyly profess a lack of interest or ability in math or business concepts. But this is not appropriate because, first, it unnecessarily diminishes their own ability, and secondly it damages the PR profession by equating it as something less than the management function it is.

A good liberal arts education is paramount to good PR practice because it ensures a person is educated in a lot of subjects and able to understand, adopt, and communicate to others a variety of concepts. Think of it this way—how can someone communicate about an environmental cause for a nonprofit if they don't have a basic understanding of ecology and biology, and how can someone advocate for a political legislation if they don't grasp the basics of government and law? In the same way, a person can not truly be a PR professional, especially not one who practices it fully as a management profession, if they have a weak or nonexistent understanding of business.

Many recent studies bear this out. Employers who hire PR professionals certainly want people who can write and communicate. But they also rank very highly something called "business acumen,"[3] which means a basic understanding of business. The two most important things employers want PR people to understand are financial statements and terminology.

Before getting into that, here is some basic advice for a PR professional when they are new to a job, or interviewing for one:

- Seek to understand exactly what the organization does. If a business, what are its products and services and how do they compare to others in that industry? If a non-profit, what is its cause and how does it address it, how is it different than other nonprofits who work on that issue?

- How does the organization make a profit or gain support? What are its primary expenses?

---

[3] Ragas, M. (2019). Defining 'business acumen': a. Delphi study of corporate communications leaders. *Public Relations Journal (13), 1.*

- What is going on broadly in business? Read major newspapers, business media, and trade publications.

Business Knowledge Basics

Business does not have to be overwhelming. A PR professional does not have to BE an economist or accountant; they only need to understand the basic principles and documents. This chapter will go over the basics of economics, finance, accounting, and intangible assets. The basics will be addressed by defining terms and illustrating common statements.

Economics

Generally, the term "**macroeconomics**" refers to the economy as a whole, whereas "**microeconomics**" refers to the effect on individuals and households. It is important to understand what perspective is employed when speaking about economic factors.

The principle of **supply and demand** is a common economic principle. Supply is how much of a product or service is available, and demand is how much people want it. If supply matches demand closely the economy is said to be in **equilibrium**. If there is more supply than demand, the price goes down, and if there is more demand than supply, the price goes up.

Horizontal and vertical integration has to do with how much of the scope of production is controlled by a business. Horizontal integration (think left and right) means a company owns different providers of parts at the same level of a supply chain or different brands of products. For example, when a national brand hotel acquires another brand hotel. Vertical (think up and down) integration means a business owns and operates several levels of a product's development, from raw materials to manufacturing to distribution. For example, if Apple made the glass and chips for its iPhone, assembled them, and sold them itself in stores and online.

Integration can lead to efficiencies and greater market share. But integration can also lead to complexities in branding.

The economy is also measured and said to be doing well or poorly. These measures are called **economic indicators**. They include:

- GDP—Gross Domestic Product, is the market value of all goods and services produced in a country in a given time period;

- Recession—"contraction" of the economy for 2 consecutive quarters;

- Employment report—tracks employment and unemployment. A good source is the Bureau of Labor Statistics;

- Consumer Price Index (CPI) is a measure of average prices of consumer goods (note—it does not include gas and groceries!);

- Interest rates—affect price and availability of credit to buy cars, homes, etc. Affect prices of bonds and stocks. Can impact individuals as well as businesses;

- Consumer Confidence—measures people's feelings vs actual data and numbers. How people feel, intend to buy, etc. For example, the Consumer Sentiment Index done by the University of Michigan;

- Currency exchange rates—the value of the US dollar to other national currencies such as the Yen, Deutschmark, Euro, Peso, Colones, etc.;

- Federal Reserve—a government agency with a dual mandate to maintain maximum employment and stable prices. They set economic policy such as federal interest rates.

Finance and the Stock Market

Finance is an important function of a business, particularly public companies that sell stocks to shareholders. Chapter 7 covers investor relations in detail, but for here the basic terminology of the stock market and finance concepts is explained.

- Bond issuance = borrowing money from investors for company use, paid back at interest rate;

- Stocks = sell "shares" of a company to investors, who are owners until they sell the shares. May pay dividend, or an amount per share based on profits;

- Liquidity = available cash (assets not tied up in stocks, bonds, or assets);

- Private or closely held = none or few shareholders, respectively;

- Futures = contract that specifies delivery of an asset on a specific date at specific price and quantity

- Option = gives option but not obligation to buy ("call") or sell ("put") a security at a specific date and price;

- IPO (Initial Public Offering) = first time offering stock. Must follow specific process of the Securities and Exchange Commission;

- EDGAR (Electronic Data Gathering, Analysis and Retrieval) is where public companies file financial information and the public can access them via www.sewc.gov;

Accounting and Financial Statements

Anyone in management , including public relations professionals, will at some point be handed financial information or statements. This can look daunting, but a basic understanding of financial information is useful. Professional accountants will prepare the documents—public relations professionals need to know how to read them.

It is important to know if an organization operates on a calendar or fiscal year. A calendar year is simply January through December. But a fiscal year could begin on June 1, October 1 or some other point during the year. This will mean a "first quarter" and so forth would include a different three months than January-March.

Accountants follow rules for how financial information is presented. These come from organizations like the Financial Accounting Standards Board (FASB) which includes Generally Accepted Accounting Principles (GAAP).

There are three main types of financial statements:

1. An **income statement** reports profit and loss (and is therefore called a "P&L"), tracks what a company made or lost/spent over a period of time;

   Key metrics on an income statement include (with formulas):

Apple Inc.

CONSOLIDATED STATEMENTS OF OPERATIONS

(In millions, except number of shares which are reflected in thousands and per share amounts)

	Years ended		
	September 30, 2017	September 24, 2016	September 26, 2015
Net sales	$ 229,234	$ 215,639	$ 233,715
Cost of sales	141,048	131,376	140,089
Gross margin	88,186	84,263	93,626
Operating expenses:			
Research and development	11,581	10,045	8,067
Selling, general and administrative	15,261	14,194	14,329
Total operating expenses	26,842	24,239	22,396
Operating income	61,344	60,024	71,230
Other income/(expense), net	2,745	1,348	1,285
Income before provision for income taxes	64,089	61,372	72,515
Provision for income taxes	15,738	15,685	19,121
Net income	$ 48,351	$ 45,687	$ 53,394

Income statement

- Gross profit = net revenue - cost of goods sold

- Operating income = net revenue - operating expenses

- Net income = net revenue - expenses

- Operating margin = operating income/net revenue

- Earnings per share = net income/total shares outstanding

Note that income is net profit or what remains after deducting expenses, while revenue is all funds received.

2. A **balance sheet** shows *assets* (what an organization owns) and *liabilities* (what an organization owes) and net worth at a given point in time. Everything must balance;

   Key metrics on a balance sheet might include:

- Total assets = total liabilities + shareholders' equity

- Shareholders' equity = total assets - total liabilities

3. **Cash flow** is a statement that shows the amount of cash generated or spent over time (not value of assets, just cash).

Other forms of financial metrics or valuation include:

- Market capitalization = stock price x current shares outstanding

- Price to Earnings Ratio (P/E) = stock price/ earnings per share

Non-financial Indicators and Intangible Assets

In addition to all the numbers and formulas above, when management talks about the business or organization they also talk about things of value that can't be measured in numbers or money, or that are invisible or intangible. It has been estimated that 80% of the stock market value of the S&P 500 companies is in intangible assets. Also, 35% of an investor's decision to invest in a company is based on non financial information about the company.

XYZ COMPANY
Balance Sheet
12/31/2017

ASSETS	
Current Assets:	
Cash	$12,000
Accounts Receivable	35,000
Inventory	120,000
Prepaid Rent	8,000
Total Current Assets	$175,000
Long-Term Assets	
Land	$126,000
Buildings & Improvements	300,000
Furniture & Fixtures	50,000
General Equipment	125,000
Total Fixed Assets	$601,000
TOTAL ASSETS	**$776,000**
LIABILITIES	
Current Liabilities:	
Accounts Payable	$60,000
Taxes Payable	25,000
Salaries/Wages Payable	30,000
Interest Payable	25,000
Total Current Liabilities	$140,000
Long Term Liabilities:	
Loan 1	$322,000
Total Long Term Liabilities	$322,000
TOTAL LIABILITIES	**$462,000**
OWNER'S EQUITY	
Paid in Capital	$64,000
Retained Earnings	250,000
TOTAL OWNER'S EQUITY	**$314,000**
TOTAL LIABILITIES & OWNER'S EQUITY	**$776,000**

Balance sheet

There are 6 categories of nonfinancial indicators. Consider how much PR has a role in developing and communicating these things:

1. Vision and strategy of company;

2. Management characteristics;

3. Employees morale and engagement (which leads to performance);

4. Reputation, brands, relationships;

5. Research and development of new products, services (R&D)

6. CSR, Corporate Social Responsibility, also called ESG—Environment, Social, Governance—factors.

Business and Communication

The business concepts above overlap. Not only should PR professionals be able to state how what they do affects the "bottom line" (meaning the net profit on the bottom line of a financial statement), but also how PR can contribute to CSR and other valuable aspects of an organization.

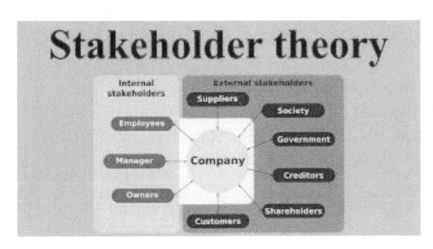

Stakeholder Theory is a perspective that is consistent with the fact that public relations works to provide positive relationships between an organization and all of its publics. These publics are called stakeholders because they all have a stake in the success or failure of the organization. They may or may not have a direct financial relationship with the organization, but if not tended to, there could be negative financial implications.

The degree to which a company is publicly valued by its CSR has increased in recent years. Triple bottom line reporting, which means reporting not just on profits but also about people and place (diversity and environmental responsibility) are expected. These are called the 3 Ps of the triple bottom line. Sometimes these are called "sustainability" annual reports.

Such communication of business activity is encouraged by:

• The Global Reporting Initiative

• The Dow Jones Sustainability Index, which tracks stocks that meet sustainability standards

• CSRWire, which carries news of the sustainable activities of companies.

A final note about intangible and non-financial assets has to do with reputation. It is hard to put reputation on a balance sheet, but it certainly can affect the financial well-being of an organization.

It's important to note the distinction between image and reputation:

• An *image* can be created and communicated and not genuine, it can be what a company merely says;

• A *reputation* is based on the public's experience with what a company does.

Reputation has become so important that there are companies, such as RepTrak, that help companies know their reputation. Each year, companies are ranked by reputation and these rankings are made public such as by the Harris Poll's annual reputation rankings.

Not only can PR professionals contribute to the management of an organization with better understanding of business terminology, PR can also show its value to management with the relational nature of the profession that lends itself to earning positive reputation and practicing CSR. Both are consistent with and the result of two-way symmetrical public relations.

For more about business and communications, consider the book "Business Essentials for Strategic Communicators" by Matt Ragas and Ron Culp.

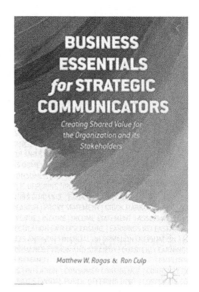

CHAPTER 3: THE PR PROCESS

Public relations professionals and students from good programs know very well that there is a process by which public relations campaigns or communication planning is done. The terms and acronyms vary from RPIE (Research, Planning, Implementation, Evaluation) to ROPES (Research, Objectives, Programming, Evaluation and Stewardship).

Another common acronym taught in textbooks as well as in professional accreditation processes is RACE—Research, Action Plan, Communication, and Evaluation. This book will follow the RACE process throughout.

Note that for the A step—Action Plan—there are sub-parts. A good action plan includes:

- Situation analysis (based on the research, defining the problem or opportunity, segmenting publics)

- Objectives

- Strategies

- Tactics

- Calendar

- Budget

- Evaluation Method

This book will focus on the objectives, strategies and tactics aspect of the action plan. Note that the prescribed process is often seen as an ideal, and there may be barriers to executing strictly according to this process. For example, a client may not want to spend the time or money to do research well, or a boss does not seem to appreciate the way evaluation was done. Nevertheless, professionals should aspire to practice according to this process.

This chapter will expand and review on each step of the process generally.

Research

Doing public relations without having done research is like going on a road trip without a map. Research is not a burden that has to be endured before getting to the "fun" and creative part of public relations. Good research helps make informed decisions, provide rationale to management, set benchmarks and provide rationale to management for whatever is proposed.

What to research

There are many things that can be researched. In general they include:

- The *publics*. A key principle is that the more narrowly segmented the public, the more precise the message, and the more effective the campaign. It is important to first find out who the relevant publics are by their interest, demographics, psychographics, past behavior and so forth. Then it is important to learn as much as possible about their characteristics, location, communication preferences and whatever else will help tailor a campaign to them.

There are several ways to think about publics. One is simply the nature of the relationship a group of people has with an organization. The bulk of this book has chapters devoted to individual publics conceived of in this way, although each can be further broken down into sub-publics.

Another way to think about publics is the distinction between audiences, stakeholders, and publics. In this way, groups of people have been considered both for the reason they are drawn together and how they act toward an organization[4]. In this sense an *audience* connects to a *message* and reacts to it. A *stakeholder* connects to an *organization* to help sustain it. A *public* connects to an *issue* to affect change.

One more way to conceive of publics is based on their level of knowledge about an organization and the degree of their involvement with it. In this view, there are five types of publics:

---

[4] *Rawlins, B. (2006) Prioritizing stakeholders for public relations. Institute for Public Relations. InstituteforPR.org*

- Aware publics—who have high knowledge but low involvement;

- Aroused publics—who have low knowledge but high involvement;

- Active publics—who have high knowledge and high involvement;

- Inactive publics—who have low knowledge and low involvement;

- Non publics—who have NO knowledge and NO involvement.[5]

- *Benchmarks*. A benchmark is a current measurement of sales, donations, inquiries, attendance, positive attitude or whatever else is relevant to a particular campaign. A benchmark is what the measure is before a campaign, and that allows for setting measurable objectives and evaluation of a campaign when it is done.

- The *problem or opportunity*. Often assumptions are made about a situation an organization faces. It could be described, for example, as a lack of awareness when in fact the target public is aware but just has a negative attitude. Researching the real problem, or framed positively as an opportunity, will help to prevent an entire campaign being focused on the wrong assumptions.

- The *competition*, or best practice research. We don't communicate in a vacuum. The publics we want to reach are probably receiving messages from competing companies, nonprofits or other entities. Best practice research means looking at good examples of how others (competitors or others) have done something that the organization now needs to do.

- The *client or organization*. Sometimes in large organizations there is useful information that can be found from documents or interviewing people. You can learn about organizational history or current information that will inform the campaign at hand.

[5] Hallahan, K. (2000). Inactive publics: The forgotten publics in public relations. *Public Relations Review* (26), 4, 499-515.

- *SWOT analysis*. This is a form of presenting research according to strengths, weaknesses, opportunities and threats. The idea is to lay out weaknesses and threats and try to mitigate them, and work to leverage strengths and opportunities.

How to research

There are various forms of research that can inform a PR campaign or program. One is available data, either from an organization's own data collected from web sites, blogs, social media or other incoming information. There are also third-party sites that have available data, such as the Census Bureau and other reports. This is a form of secondary research, which could include internet searches and library searches on key words and topics.

Qualitative research, such as focus groups, can yield deep insights about opinions, attitudes, and behaviors from a sample of a target public. Done well, a focus group or depth interviews is very valid and accurate knowledge, but it is not possible to generalize to an entire population. Nevertheless, qualitative data is helpful to avoid making assumptions or guessing about a public.

Surveys are a popular form of primary research. If constructed well and randomly served to a larger sample of a target public, surveys can statistically be generalized to the target public population at large with greater confidence. Sometimes focus groups and surveys are done, with the former used to derive specific questions that are posed to larger sample for whom the questions will make more sense.

Objectives

Objectives are a way to articulate the reason a PR campaign is being done. There are two general types of objectives, one is desired and one is not. An *output* objective is one that sets a goal for what the PR professional will do, or put out. An example output objective is: "distribute 1,000 brochures to potential customers in the week before the store opens.:" Again, that really is stating what the PR pro will do in the campaign and is technically only a tactic which comes later.

An *outcome* objective by comparison is what a savvy PR professional should use. It is about what the public does in response to the campaign. An outcome could be a change in the target public awareness, attitude, or action—called the "3 As" of outcome objectives.

Outcome objectives should be written as a concise, clear statement that has four parts:

• One public

• One outcome (awareness, attitude, action)

• A measure, in terms of a number or percentage to be achieved

• A time by which the outcome will be achieved.

For example, a good outcome objective would be:

"increase awareness of the new store by 75% among women aged 35-50 in River City by October 30, 2020."

Look at the example again with the four parts identified:

"increase awareness (outcome) of the new store by 75% (measure) among women aged 35-50 in River City (public) by October 30, 2020 (time)."

An example *attitude* objective might be:

"increase to 50% the number of customers who indicate the store is their preferred brand in this market by November 30, 2020."

An example *action* objective might be:

"increase by 25% the number of women aged 35-50 who purchase from the store by December 31, 2020."

Here are a few more tips for writing clear objectives:

- Do NOT include a tactic in an objective. For example, don't say: "Distribute 1,000 brochures so that...." (typically, if an objective includes the words "so that" it is bad form and includes a tactic, which should be saved for later in the plan.

- Do not include more than one public in an objective. For example, don't say: "increase awareness of men and women by ...." Different publics may react differently and must be measured separately, therefore write a separate objective for each public.

- Do not have more than one outcome in the same objective. For example, do not say "increase awareness of and attitude about..." Again, separate objectives happen at different rates and need to be stated and measured separately.

- When it comes to setting measurable objectives, keep in mind that awareness is easiest to achieve, changing attitude somewhat more challenging, and motivating to action the most difficult. So a higher number makes sense for awareness, a lower number for attitude, and the lowest for action. A good rule of thumb is to be reasonable in expectations.

- Also remember to base objectives off the benchmark (current number) found in research. An objective can be stated as an increase from a benchmark (eg: increase by 20%...") or an attained level as a number or percentage if no benchmark could be determined because the organization or product is new (eg: "obtain 55 referrals...." Or "achieve 75% positive reviews....)

- A helpful formula for how many objectives to have would be: total number of publics x total number of outcomes = total number of objectives for a campaign. So if a campaign has three age groups each of of men and women in a city, that would be six publics. It depends on how many ways a public is segmented. If there is a need to change awareness, attitude, and action for each public, that would be a total of 18 objectives (6 publics x 3 outcomes each). If there are only two publics, say residents of two different cities, and the only outcome desired is an action, then it would be 2 publics by 1 outcome so 2 objectives.

Strategy

Recall from the earlier chapter that a strategy is purposeful and tied to the overall mission of an organization. Looking more closely at strategy in the context of a campaign, it can also be said that a strategy can come in a variety of forms.

A strategy could be simply in how the publics are *segmented*, or on which people a campaign will focus. This is far more strategic than scattershot communications to an ill-defined "general public."

Example public segmentation strategy: target fathers of young children.

Another strategy could be in terms of *timing*. A message about summer vacation sent in July would be too late. A message to college seniors about job search services in the beginning of their senior year would be more strategic because that would be when the target public would be thinking about such things.

Example timing strategy: reach out in early spring when families are planning summer activities.

The application of communication or persuasive theory, also known as the appeal, is the most compelling and effective strategy. Going beyond just sharing facts is necessary to get attention, change minds, and motivate to action. This is an aspect of creativity, writing and communication that answers not just "what" in a message but "why" and "how." This is also where research on the public and problem can be applied.

Example appeal strategy: address their fear of failure by stressing their self-efficacy in using this program.

There are dozens of strategies and they can not all be categorized or listed here. As a rule of thumb, if you can not explain to a colleague or client why something you propose will work, you likely do not have a strategy. If you can confidently provide rationale and expectations for an idea, you have a strategy.

Tactics

Tactics are merely tangible communication tools or channels. While some think PR is about media relations, that is just one tool. In fact, any potential communication tactic could be part of a PR campaign. This could be anything in what has been called the PESO model (Paid, Earned, Shared and Owned). This is a modern depiction of what was once called a "media mix."

In subsequent chapters, more information will be provided on tactics that may be unique to reaching the public of focus for the chapter. But there are a host of general tactics for PR campaigns that may apply to multiple publics. Arranged according to the PESO model, these include:

- Paid—any advertisements in print, broadcast, outdoor or digital form.

- Earned—news releases, pitches, tip sheets, editorials and other tactics used in reaching journalists or communicating through news media.

- Shared—web sites, blogs, social media and tactics that can be shared by users to reach multiple networks of people.

- Owned—tactics that an organization "owns" and controls, beyond shared described above. These include brochures, newsletters, annual reports, direct mail, events, and more.

Evaluation

Evaluation may sound difficult, but in principle is is easy:

Did the campaign meet its objectives?

That's it! Look at the objectives stated earlier, and measure to see if they were met or not. This can be done by observed measure (attendance at events, responses to direct mail, an observable increase in sales) or by evaluative research such as a post campaign focus group or survey, social media sentiment and digital analytics.

The Barcelona Principles depicted on the next page are international standards for evaluating public relations.

Some have pointed out that public relations is about *relationships*. The question becomes, how can relationships between an organization and its publics be measured? Academics have studied this and determined four variables make up relationships. They can be measured through a survey to key publics asking them to respond to a set of statements on a 5- or 7-point Likert-type scale (strongly agree, agree, neutral, disagree, strongly disagree). The four relationship variables are:

- Trust—the degree to which a person trusts the organization and what they say and do;

- Satisfaction—the degree to which a person is satisfied with interactions and communication with the organization;

- Commitment—the degree to which a person believes the organization cares about and is committed to their well-being and not just organization self interest;

- Control mutuality—the degree to which a person believes they have as much control over interactions as the organization, can start conversations, raise concerns, and get a response.

All of the above of course lead to positive *reputation*. To sum up the parts of the PR process:

- **Research** =segments and identifies public(s) characteristics, yields benchmark or current measure;

- **Objective** = sets goal of how to move that measure or number, either increase or decrease, number or percent;

- **Strategies** = the method by which the public will be likely to do what the objective is, usually in terms of segmenting, timing, and message appeal;

- **Tactics** = the specific communication tools;

- **Evaluation = looks at whether stated objectives were met or exceeded or not.**

Part II covers a set of specific publics with whom public relations professionals may seek to build and maintain relationships on behalf of an organization. Each public will be considered in terms of the unique types of research, objectives, strategies, tactics, and evaluation that apply.

Part II: Publics

This section will devote a chapter to each of several specific publics. Each chapter is organized according to the PR process, spelling out unique aspects of research, objectives, strategies, tactics and evaluation for each public.

CHAPTER 4: EMPLOYEE RELATIONS

Some might consider employees to be only the concern of human resources. And that is certainly the focus of that management function. But a public relations professional has good reason to consider employees and a significant role to play from a management perspective.

Consider that employees may affect all external communications, particularly if they communicate with external publics as part of their own job function. Also, these days, many CEOs and others in management say attracting and retaining "talent" (a buzz word for skilled employees) is one of their top concerns. So, potential employees and their interests and needs have to be considered. And past employees can still affect an organization's reputation.

Consider that employees, just like products, have a "life cycle" and organizations need to communicate strategically with them at each stage. This starts with a person's *perception* of an organization as a place to work before they are even considering applying, then the *hiring* process, then the *work* experience for the period of time they are actual employees, and finally the *termination*

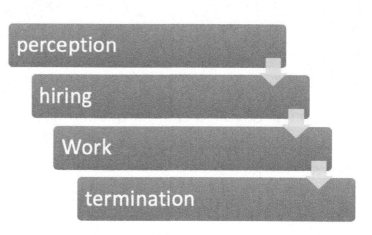

process, whether it is amiable such as retirement or transition or even it is less pleasant due to downsizing or firing.

A good employee relations program starts with how management views employees. Too often management sees employees as a cost, as in labor cost. Or they treat them as a commodity, such as human resources or labor force. It is also possible for management to look down on employees as subordinates "beneath" their level in the organization. This isn't always the case, but the attitude persists too often, with obvious consequences for the relationship between an organization and its employees.

Management	PR
Cost	Asset
Commodity	Co-owner
Subordinate	Partner

A better attitude about employees is to see them as individual human beings. If there really is a "talent" shortage, current employees should be seen as an asset, not just a cost. Management should also recognize. That. Employees are stakeholders since their job is their livelihood. Some companies actually have formalized employee ownership programs. Finally, management should see employees as having different roles but still being partners in the organization's mission.

Views of Employees

In short, consider all of what communication to employees can affect, either positively or negatively. Taking employee communication seriously can create the good things on this list and prevent the bad ones:

- Morale

- Loyalty

- Attendance

- Work quality; customer satisfaction

- Word of mouth; reputation

- Recruiting

- Unionizing, arbitration

- Lawsuits

Research

There are a number of things to research about employees, and some standard ways to do it. Employee satisfaction is a common metric in employee relations. This is most often done with anonymous surveys. Part of such a survey can also measure positive or negative sentiment about specific aspects of the organization and work culture, as well as general morale or mood of employees about being associated with the organization.

The research should uncover facts about employee satisfaction with their specific job and the tasks they do. But it should also get at their attitudes about communication, what is shared, how, how often, and by whom. Employees can interpret poor communication as a lack of respect for them, which leads to a culture problem. On that note, it is important to solicit input and ideas from employees, which is both good research as well as smart strategy to gain their sense of belonging.

Finally, by observation the turnover rate should be studied. If employees come and go frequently, that's a sign of a bad employee atmosphere and results in costs of recruiting and retraining employees as opposed maintaining a happy, productive workforce that represents the organization well.

Objectives

The objectives for employee relations boil down to hiring good employees, keeping them a long time, and helping them to be happy and productive in their jobs. These objectives fall into the following categories, with specific objectives written as described in the chapter 3 on process:

- Recruitment. The communication we do about a company or organization can be for a variety of purposes—branding, sales, fundraising and more. But potential employees are seeing this communication as well, and it is important to be mindful of that. At the same time, being intentional about getting not just someone to fill a position but the *best* candidate should be the objective so an organization is competitive, not just operational. Working to be the company or organization in your industry that is the "employer of choice" is a good objective. In other words, given a choice of where to work, employees want to work for you, either right now or down the road when they are looking for the next job. It's called being top of mind in employee recruitment.

- Retention. Once employees are on board, the goal is to keep them. Retention is the opposite of turnover and should be planned for with intent.

- Productivity. We also want employees to be productive, which means different things depending on their jobs. Essentially, it means successful in their job, and growing in their ability through ongoing training, development, and promotions.

- Loyalty. Many PR professionals talk about the advantage of having "brand ambassadors," which means people speaking positively on behalf of an organization even though it is not their job in particular. People are often asked where they work and how they like it. It should be a goal that they answer that type of question positively. Also, employees should be informed of organizational plans, intentions, and other facts so they can speak up to friends, on social media and elsewhere to promote initiatives or correct misperceptions. Again, employees should be seen as assets and should be enabled as such.

Strategies

If retention is a goal, then treating employees in a way that makes them want to stay is an obvious strategy. The graphic below illustrates some reasons employees stay with their current job and employer:

Potential employees pay a lot of attention to what current employees have to say about their work experience—everything from pay to job duties to how they are communicated to.

Empowerment is an important strategy in employee communications. That means giving employees a sense of control and power over their own jobs, a defined role in the company, and letting them know how their job contributes to the overall organizational success. This can take different forms given that some jobs may be menial, such as factory work, and others more akin to what is known as "information workers" of office jobs. But either way, all employees have value and perspective, and demonstrating that by empowering them to offer ideas can be beneficial to an organization in terms of getting those good ideas but also building morale and keeping employees.

With regard to empowerment, it is important to think of power more broadly. Power is often perceived to be a finite concept, that if a manager gives an employee some power, then the manager has less. But the opposite is true—giving an employee a sense of power actually bolsters a manager's power in the way they are viewed and supported by employees and in the collective power of working collaboratively. Also, power comes in different forms, in what theorists call power "currencies". In other words the American dollar and the British pound are different currencies but both are money. Power is the same in that it can be in the form of authority, expertise, experience, charisma and more. In this way, managers and employees both have power, albeit of different kinds, and instead of seeing empowerment as a threat, managers should see it as a strategy to accomplish organizational objectives.

Employee engagement is a category of strategies that can be effective in yielding positive results. Engagement essentially means dialogue and conversation with employees in an ongoing fashion. Research[6] has shown that employee engagement won't

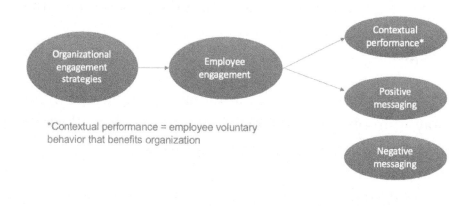

[6] •From "Engaged at Work? An Employee Engagement Model in Public Relations" by Shen and Jiang (2019, Vol 31, ½, pp 32-49)

happen without a defined strategy to do so, and that the benefits of employee engagement include employees taking initiative to benefit an organization and engage in their own positive messaging about the company. Strategies to stimulate engagement include openness, networking within the organization, and providing assurance that employee concerns and ideas are legitimate.

Culture is another consideration when it comes to strategy for employee relations. This is another topic that CEOs say they worry or think about often. That's because a culture is a perceived, shared set of values that guide behavior. A good culture means people "automatically" do the right thing, and a bad culture means it is a constant challenge to improve employee attitudes and behaviors.

Culture can also be considered a set of norms, or unwritten rules. When someone says "that's just the way we do things here," they are describing their culture whether they know it or not. Organizations should be intentional about culture with new employees through training and "onboarding" programs. Here is the key—cultures are best established, communicated and perpetuated through "stories." Stories have heroes, people who are praised and therefore emulated for their behavior. So, a key would be in all employee communications—speeches, newsletters, intranet and more—that PR professionals don't just send information, they tell stories.

David Friedman[7] worked in a variety of organizations and now consults with those who want to improve their culture for employees. He recommends 8 steps:

1. Define the employee behaviors that lead to success

2. Ritualize the behaviors through intentional repetition

3. Select employees who fit the culture, and fire those who don't!

4. Integrate employees into the culture right away (first impressions)

5. Communicate the culture with visible reminders in many tactics

---

[7] ●"Culture by Design: 8 Simple Steps to Drive Better Individual and Organizational Performance" by David Friedman

6. Coach to reinforce behaviors that drive culture

7. Lead the culture by example (leaders DO don't just say)

8. Drive culture with accountability (performance reviews, etc)

Tactics

When it comes to tactics for employee relations, they include all of the usual possibilities. Town hall and other meetings where a leader gives a speech in a personal and relatable way is a good idea. Internal newsletters, intranets, and even bulletin boards, posters and signs can be effective.

There are also a number of tech tools that work well with employees. Yammer is a form of Twitter for internal audiences only. The employee app is a way to engage with employees in an application that can be tailored to an organization. Facebook Workplace has become popular as a collaborative communication tool, as has Slack. There are others as well. It's best to explore and find the one that is most appropriate for an organization, and that includes one that employees are able to adopt and interested in using.

Evaluation

There are various ways to evaluate employee relations. Remember, the evaluation should seek to determine if the employee relations objectives are being met. Since organizations are ongoing, this evaluation should happen regularly, at least annually if not more frequently.

One form of evaluation is to monitor media commentary with regard to the organization's culture or employee satisfaction. Many business and other publications do annual lists of "best places to work." Being on such a list is a good measure of successful employee relations because they are often based on employee feedback and other objective measures.

One source of data used in those articles is Glassdoor, an open site where employees from any organization can anonymously share sentiments about their jobs. Many potential employees look there before applying for jobs.

Finally, there is primary research that can be used to evaluate employee relations objectives. This could include:

- Employee satisfaction surveys. These can be done quarterly or annually.

- Informal and formal feedback. Listen to employees, share what they say with other managers. Ignoring such organic evaluation is unwise and leads to problems.

- Performance reviews. Keep in mind that employees should also be able to evaluate their supervisors. This sends a message that they are valued and also yields helpful information. The best practice is to evaluate employees in terms of how well they demonstrate organizational values, as well as simple job tasks.

- Hiring interviews. Build good questions into job interviews to learn about potential employee perceptions of the organization, why they want to work there, what they have heard from other employees. This helps make hiring decisions but also is an evaluation of employee relations.

- Exit interviews. Not many organizations do this. But if an employee leaves for whatever reason, it is good to do an exit interview after a little time has passed. This makes the conversation less awkward and more confidential. Sometimes this information can be unpleasant, but it may be valuable to change internal communications and prevent further departures of good employees who did not feel informed, valued or treated well enough to stay.

CHAPTER 5: COMMUNITY RELATIONS

Community relations is a public relations function that can be ignored all together, but some organizations do it extremely well. Other publics may be more obvious because they have a direct and often financial relationship with an organization. A community is either geographical, as in the residents of a city where an organization has a facility or does its work, or topical, in the case of online or other communities based on common interest.

Nevertheless, communities however defined are also stakeholders, in the sense that they have a stake in the success of an organization. Maybe they indirectly benefit in terms of tax base, employment provided, or the positive impact of whatever an organization's mission is. But the benefit of community relations is mutual, as is made clear in this definition:

> As a public relations function, **community relations** is an organization's planned, active, and continuing participation within a community to maintain and enhance its environment, to the benefit of the organization, its employees and other stakeholders, and the larger community.

Some organizations have departments or individual job titles called community relations, or the function is part of the job description of a public relations generalist. But if a CEO or another executive needs convincing that community relations is important, they only need to be told what community relations—or the lack of it—could affect:

- Community "goodwill". As pointed out in the chapter on business, goodwill is almost like having something in the bank. An organization never knows when it will need community support for a building project, a fundraising campaign, or another initiative. Goodwill or positive perception of the organization within a community can also be beneficial in the following situations;

- Local laws and regulations such as zoning or ballot initiatives will be more favorable and supported if relationships with the community are good;

- Employee recruitment—as noted in the previous chapter, finding good employees is an ongoing objective. Good community relations positions an organization as a place local residents may desire to work;

- Local sales or donor support can be better if an organization is involved with a community at large;

- Investors, volunteers, other publics could all live in community and they witness and are influenced by the way an organization interacts with the community;

- An ethical imperative driven by Stakeholder Theory to be concerned for the well-being of all publics.

The "community" can include many publics, such as some listed in the bullet points above. Others include government officials, opinion leaders, business partners and suppliers, physical neighbors and more. Relationships of mutual understanding with all these community publics contributes to organizational success.

Research

Research in community relations involves finding out more about the community (or in the case of national or regional organizations, several communities where an organization has a presence). This means first determining who the specific publics are within a community. It is not strategic but sloppy PR to simply target the "general community." It's better to do some research and find a more specific set of publics with whom the organization does or should have relationship to build mutual awareness and understanding.

The second area of research is to find out what are the specific needs of a specific community. Some community relations programs just barge in with a philanthropic gift or local program without consulting the community first, and this can come off more as arrogant than helpful. Communities are not all the same, and have a wide variety of different needs given their context. Here are a few categories of community needs:

- Employment opportunity

- Growth of local economy

- Adequate competitive businesses to provide consumer choice

- Competent municipal government and services

- Education, religion, recreation

- Housing and public service

- Legal, medical, other professional services

- Pride and loyalty

- Good reputation in the region and state

Objectives

The objectives of community relations are numerous but tend to fall into these categories:

- Reputation as good 'corporate citizen' or admired nonprofit;

- Recognition or awareness for presence in community and knowledge about what the organization does;

- Support of community for other objectives;

- To be seen as community resource or asset.

Strategies

In terms of strategy, community relations can be thought of in several ways., The first is why to do it, or how community relations contributes to overall organizational objectives. The second is how to go about it.

With regard to why to do community relations, there are three strategic answers: defensive, proactive, or maintenance. A defensive strategy would be to prevent negative acts or the perception that the organization does not care. Good community relations makes it harder for the community to accuse the organization of something. A proactive strategy would be to conduct community relations as a form of social branding or demonstrating organizational "purpose," which is increasingly expected of organizations. This can position an organization as a thought leader beyond its own mission and on social issues. A maintenance strategy means working to keep growing the positive relationships, reputation and word of mouth about the organization. It is not possible to rest on organizational success—it's an ongoing effort to maintain.

When planning how to do community relations, there are two strategies[8]. One has been called "episodic" which means doing community relations on occasion and keeping the community at an "arms length" from the organization. Such efforts are short term, and necessarily can yield only short term or minimal benefits or even backfire as a community thinks the effort is not genuine but conditional on getting something in return.

Nevertheless, here are some examples of community relations activities that are episodic:

• Management serves on local boards;

• Speakers bureau, a list of organization employees who can speak to local groups;

• Open house, an event in the organization's facility;

• Allow use of facilities;

• Participate in or sponsor local events.

The other way to do community relations strategically is "relational," or within the fabric of the community. This is more of a long-term prospect, done with a sustained relationship in mind, and it yields more social capital or mutual benefit. It also takes more investment and planning and resources by the organization.

Examples of relational community relations activities include:

8 *Johnson, K. & Lane, A. (2018) Building relational capital: The contribution of episodic and relational community engagement. Public Relations Review (44), 633-644.*

- Advisory boards, in which members of the community advise the organization;

- Opinion leaders in community, meaning employees of the organization serve as opinion leaders and resources on community issues;

- Employee volunteer programs, in which employees can suggest initiatives and are given work-release time to do projects that benefit the community;

- Community research, or offering the resources of the organization to gather and report data to local government and other organizations who would benefit from it;

- Local philanthropy, such as giving grants or sponsorships to enable local teams, clubs and new organizations to emerge and sustain themselves.

Several other strategic considerations must be determined. Should the organization participate in the initiative or lead it? Should the community involvement be determined by management or the employees? Who will the community partners be and how will they be selected?

Tactics

All of the strategic ways to engage in the community listed above need to be communicated somehow. The question is always whether community relations should be done humbly and allow others to praise an organization, or if the organization should tout its own work in the community.

A combination would work best, and the issue may be the tone with which an organization does it. It should not be boastful and arrogant, but a simple expression of what is done and the reason the organization does it. Often it can be tied to organizational mission, part of its purpose, an expression that owners and employees are also members of the community, or some other acceptable reason for sharing community relations plans and progress.

The tactics could include news releases, ads, newsletter articles, social media engagement, or even a dedicated community impact annual report. The various strategic ways of doing community relations also can double as tactics, such as the sponsorship of a little league team, or a volunteering event with employees.

Evaluation

As always, evaluation of community relations should be a measure of whether community relations objectives were met. But generally speaking, community relations can be measured by keeping tabs on sentiment in the community via letters to the editor, social media comments and mentions, and direct communication in the form of thanks.

Another measure could be a more formal and intentional community perception survey, to assess if the community and key publics within it are aware of and think positively about the organization's community relations efforts.

Additionally, an organization can quantify money raised and given, the number of volunteers or volunteer hours, the number of community partners, attendance at events, participation of community members in programs and other numerical measures that can be compared to desired numbers set in objectives.

Here are two examples of community relations programs online:

- Lake Michigan Credit Union (LMCU)

- Priority Health

CHAPTER 6: GOVERNMENT RELATIONS & PUBLIC AFFAIRS

Government relations and public affairs are related and yet distinct concepts.

G•*Government relations* involves organizations reaching out to influence government officials. This is often called "lobbying," stemming from the days when people would wait in the lobby of a capitol building for legislators to emerge so they could talk to them.

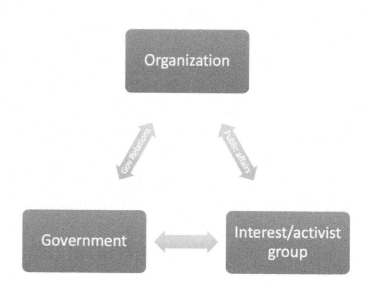

• *Public affairs* involves organizations reaching out to activist/interest groups to build or restore relationships over specific issues, and can also mean governments engaging in public information to citizens or constituents.

So the publics in this chapter are multiple. When an organization engages government officials in local, state and federal offices and agencies about pending legislation it is called government relations. When an organization engages with activist groups about an issue that has emerged it is called public affairs. The relationships can be seen in the graphic above.

Research

There are three basic things to research in government relations and public affairs—the government officials and agencies, the activist or interest group, and the issue at hand.

With government officials or agencies, much information is available online. A good starting point is https://www.usa.gov/agencies. With specific elected officials, knowing what committees they are on and their past voting records is necessary before approaching them with an argument regarding a law or policy. Also, knowing the top issues they campaigned on or care about and their stance on them and reasons for that stance can be useful. Also, knowing who supports them can be useful information in order to strategically partner in efforts to persuade a legislator.

Government agencies, such as the Federal Communications Commission (FCC) or Federal Trade Commission (FTC) and so forth all have their own web sites. Information about their appointed commissioners and all of their past and pending regulations, with rationale and research about them, is easily available.

Activist groups are harder to research. If they are well organized, such as political action groups (PACs), they may have literature about their position on issues and who their primary leaders are. Otherwise, some old-fashioned surveys and other forms of grounded research may be necessary to understand the people and their attitudes before engaging with them.

Added to the above is general public opinion research. Even if people don't identify as being part of an activist group, they may have an opinion on an issue. It is important to know where the majority stands, and also the "valence" or how strongly people hold opinions on an issue. This information is useful when it comes to strategy.

Objectives

Objectives in government relations and public affairs can be extremely action based and obvious, or they can be more subtle and relationship oriented.

One type of objective is simple to achieve a specific vote, either to pass or defeat a proposed bill or regulation. There may be other objectives along the way, such as encouraging members of the public to write or call their elected officials, attend events, request information and so on. But all of this leads to the legislative goal.

Another type of objective is education, or getting people to understand an issue and to see it as important. Then, the objectives become more about changing minds to the organization's point of view on the issue. This goes for both the identified members of an activist group as well as general public opinion.

A final type of objective is relational in nature. That means turning an activist public that may have been opposed to an organization on an issue from having a negative or hostile view of the organization to one that is more positive, or at least more neutral when considering the organization apart from the single issue that defined the group. It can also just mean gaining and maintaining public awareness and support for a cause or organization in general and not about an issue.

Strategies

Often in government relations and public affairs the root of the situation is a conflict, a disagreement in opinion about an issue and what to do about it. Therefore, conflict resolution is the approach to take, and there are typically five conflict resolution styles or strategies, each based on how active an approach is, willingness to adapt, and the degree to which the conflict is resolved.

- Avoid—no action taken and the issue is not resolved (lose-lose);

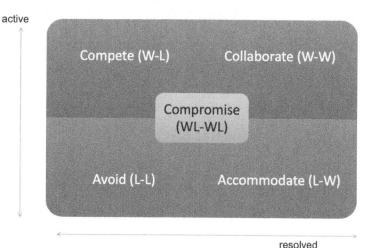

- Compete—very active, but maintain one's own position so conflict is not resolved, a win-at-all-cost approach (win-lose);

- Accommodate—not very active and give in to opposing side to resolve conflict (lose-win);

- Compromise—both sides give a little to settle the conflict (both win and lose);

- Collaborate—both sides work together to satisfactorily resolve the conflict (win-win).

Which style is chosen depends on the situation. An organization or PR professional has to ask management how much they are willing to "fight," how important the issue is to the organization, and if the relationship is more important to save or restore than to win on the issue.

Strategies in government relations often include lobbying activities. Some of this is merely gathering and presenting facts to legislators to help them make more informed decisions. Sometimes lobbying is more strategic, such as communicating about an issue in an elected official's home district or state so they are pressured by their own voters to act a certain way. In a similar fashion, building coalitions of individuals and groups is a common strategy because a greater the number of people representing a point of view will be more persuasive to a politician.

Grassroots campaigns are also a strategy. This means assembling groups of "common" everyday people into a group centered on an issue. This gains more visibility to the public at large and elected officials to gain attention and potentially change minds and actions, such as a vote. Ethically, one must be careful here to ensure such groups are legitimate and not "front groups" or "astroturf" campaigns in which it is claimed there is a group of concerned citizens when in fact they have not organized themselves as such.

There are also a variety of standard strategies for public affairs, centered on raising awareness and changing opinion about public issues and policies:

- *Frame the issue early.* Often the first person or organization to state what the issue is "really" about, or provide an emphasis, is how people will think about the issue. For example, a ban on oil drilling could be framed as environmental protection or a barrier to business.

- *Make the issue relevant to key publics.* It's not effective to just start communicating about and trying to persuade people on an issue. First, it needs to be shown to be of personal impact. For example, a tax increase for a public bus system may not seem worthwhile to a resident who has a car until it is stressed that it will decrease traffic and help the unemployed get jobs.

- *Build coalitions and allies.* As noted above, there is strength in numbers. Bi-partisan (people from both parties) is best so an issue doesn't become perceived as just Republican or Democrat.

- *Demonstrate a position is consistent with majority public opinion.* People generally like to think they are in the majority, so stating a position is in line with that can be persuasive to undecided individuals and reinforce those already in agreement.

- *Show you are not merely self-interested.* People may have a tendency to oppose organizations and businesses, especially large ones, out of resentment for their power. This is why it is important to show broad impact and benefit of a proposal or position on an issue so people understand its effect on many.

- *Target media in key lawmaker districts.* As noted above, even if a lawmaker comes from a distant state or district, they may serve on a key committee that will affect regulation of the issue of concern.

In recent years, it has become an expectation for organizations to articulate their "purpose" in terms of benefit to society and not just their own mission. This has led to pressure for organizations and their leaders to take a stand or hold a clear position one way or the other on the key issues in society. This can gain a lot of fans and supporters, but it can also lead to opposition. So whether or not and how to speak out on issues becomes a strategic concern. The emerging advice from PR professionals includes the following considerations:

1. Who are the publics engaged on this issue and are they relevant to your organization? What is their prevailing interest in and opinion on the topic?

2. Who is asking you to engage? Is it someone from your current publics, the media, or some third party?

3. How does this request to comment on an issue align with overall organizational plans and objectives?

4. Will the issue be in the public eye a long time?

5. What would happen if you did nothing?

6. How will taking a stand affect sales, donations, employment, reputation and more?

7. Does the organization actually have a strong and genuine opinion on the issue?

8. Are you prepared to defend a stance taken?

Tactics

Tactics in government relations and public affairs can include a lot of the conventional public relations tactics. But the ones used more often in this type of PR include:

- Position papers, opinion editorials, fact sheets, studies, letter-writing campaigns;

- Issue based micro-sites, or web sites specifically about an issue;

- Social media, including special issue-based groups and hashtags. Govloop is a social media platform specifically for those who work in government;

- Speeches;

- Meetings with lawmakers and "town hall" meetings with public about the issue to gain input and share perspective;

- Advertorials, or ads that read like articles, as well as issue ads;

- Public opinion surveys which are a form of research but also a tactic that informs people who receive the survey and can get them to think about it.

Evaluation

Evaluation in government relations and public affairs is, as always, about seeing if specific, measurable objectives were met. Generally speaking, such evaluation with these publics would include:

- Votes;

- Public opinion shift;

- Issue resolution;

- Specific government actions;

- Maintenance or restoration of reputation;

- Nature of relationships with politicians and interest groups.

CHAPTER 7: INVESTOR RELATIONS

Investor relations can also be called financial communications, which may be a broader term. Investors are a vital public specifically in the context of public companies who sell stock. Investors can also be called stockholders (not to be confused with stakeholders.

While stockholders invest in a company with the intent to profit through dividends paid per share of stock or subsequently selling the stock at a higher price, nonprofit organizations also have a form of investor. These are more commonly called donors, but their interest is not to profit off the investment but to see the nonprofit organization achieve its mission. In nonprofit organization the investor relations function can be called donor relations, development, or advancement. This chapter will primarily use the terms of investor relations, but many concepts can be applied to donors as well.

A working definition of investor relations is:

A strategic management responsibility, using the disciplines of finance, communication, and marketing to manage the flow of company information to financial and other constituencies to manage relative valuation.

Notice the definition speaks of blending disciplines of finance, communication and marketing. Realize that PR professionals who specialize in investor relations focus on the communication aspect and have their colleagues in finance and accounting to help with specifically financial information. But also, refer back to chapter 2 for some key business and financial terms and documents.

In focusing on communications, there are a variety of skills expected for success in investor relations. They include writing and speaking, an adequate financial knowledge and awareness of legal issues. But, management skills and the ability to work with the CEO and CFO are necessary. Understanding the company and its business as well as trends in its industry category are a must as well.

The publics in investor relations go beyond merely the investors. It's important to understand the broader investor relations landscape to do IR well. These publics include:

- Business journalists—these are the people who cover business and often their stories can be influential in whether people buy or sell stock. Specific business outlets such as CNBN, Fox Business, Forbes, Fortune and the Wall Street Journal have a national scope, but many other business media are important to work with in investor relations as well.

- Research analysts—this is a unique group of people whose job it is to write analysis reports about the merits of a company stock. Many of them specialize in a specific industry. They can really influence investors, so providing them with timely and accurate information is key.

- Institutional investors—these are people or companies who buy large quantities of stock to put in mutual funds, pensions and other pools of investments that are in turn sold to others. For example, brokers at Merrill Lynch or Fidelity, and those who manage pension funds are considered institutional investors because they invest for an institution and not as an individual. Obviously, they buy and sell large quantities of stock and communicating with them is crucial.

- Individual (retail) investors—these are the average people who buy stock either through companies like E-Trade or through a broker. There are three types of retail investors based on their actions:

  - Buy and hold—they tend to buy stock and hold on to it for a long time before selling it, usually just to grow their retirement fund;

  - Day traders—as the name implies, these people "play the market" and look to buy and then sell rapidly to make quick profits;

  - Regular reviewers—people who assess the performance of their stocks and sell or buy on a quarterly or annual basis.

Investor relations publics can also be thought of as being on the "buy side" or "sell side" of interactions. Some are on both, depending on current situations. But investor relations professionals consider them in terms of their primary behavior or the company's objective for them. Therefore, individual and institutional investors are the primary buy side publics, and analysts and brokers are primary sell side because of their ability to influence buyers of stock.

Research

Research in investor relations involves finding out who the specific publics are. Who covers the industry and a specific company in the media and among analysts? What has been the content of those articles and reports, in terms of positive or negative assessment of the company and its stock?

Other research can be done to find out who the primary investors are, what their sentiment or attitude is about the company, and what influences them most when it comes to buying stock. The most important objective of course is increasing the purchase of the stock and the stock price. Some more on investor sentiment and influences will be covered later in the chapter.

Objectives

Objectives in investor relations involve influencing the publics identified above to be aware of and have positive attitudes about the company and its stock. More specific categories of investor relations objectives are:

- Communicate company value to Wall Street. Wall Street is a shorthand for brokers and investors who buy and sell stock and the media and analysts who write about it. Essentially this is an objective for a number of positive stories and reports and attitudes about a stock being worth buying.

- Clarify growth strategy and financial performance measures. Investors look closely at company strategy to grow in terms of market expansion, number of customers, new products, sales and other measures.

- Ensure consistent communication. If there are mixed messages about a company the investors can get nervous. This is an objective about the nature of content about the company.

- Build relationships with financial opinion leaders. These opinion leaders are the analysts and brokers mentioned above.

- Assist management in compliance with SEC and other regulations. There will be a "compliance officer" at public companies, usually an accountant or financial specialist, but it is a PR issue to comply or with government regulations or a crisis will certainly follow.

- Boost stock price. This is the bottom line in investor relations. If the stock price goes down or is stagnant, there is little reason for buyers to invest.

Strategies

In thinking about investor relations strategy, it is helpful to think about what influences a stock price. A formula for stock price is P+L+P, or performance (a company's sales) plus liquidity (the company's ability to sell shares based on available shares to sell) plus perception (the reputation of a company and the value of its stock). The third is the one that can most be influenced by PR, but the first two are factors that can be addressed in communications as well.

Messaging strategy is most important in investor relations, and many messages are the business indicators discussed in chapter 2. Financial message strategies often are about stressing the stock price track over time and the P/E ratio, the profit or loss and quarterly and annual earnings, and the amount of dividend to be paid per share.

Giving an "early warning" is a common strategy. This means communicating negative news before the required quarterly report comes out with specific numbers about sales and other financial data. It lets investor publics know that the company did not meet expectations before the details come out and prevents a shock in the market.

Another strategy is whether a stock is positioned as growth or value. Many of them are labeled as such by analysts and stock ratings companies like morningstar.com . A growth stock is one that has good potential to increase in price in the coming quarters or years, so even if the stock price is currently high investors may still buy because the price will go even higher. A value stock is one with a low price and could lead people to think it is not worth considering, but it is called value because it is considered priced lower than it is worth, thus encouraging investors to buy it.

Chapter 2 discussed non financial indicators, and it can be a strategy to mention and stress these in communications too. Studies have shown[9] that investors are influenced by a range of nonfinancial indicators that include:

- The quality of individual members of management, including the CEO, other officers, and who is on the board;

- The strategy of the company to grow and profit;

- The types and quality of products and services;

- The nature of the market in terms of risk and potential;

- Organizational capital, or the amount of cash the company has to use to expand and improve its operations and products;

- The quality of overall corporate communications;

- R&D, or what research and development is ongoing that could lead to breakthrough products that would drive profits;

- Employees, in terms of their talent and abilities as well as how well they are treated and retained;

- CSR. Many investors make stock buying decisions in consideration of how "good" a company is socially and in terms of its responsibility.

In terms of nonprofits, many of the above that apply are also important to donors so worth including strategically in communications to influence donors. In

[9] Penning, T. (2011) "The Value of Public Relations in Investor Relations: Individual Investors' Preferred Information Types, Qualities, and Sources." Journalism & Mass Communication Quarterly (88), 3, pp.615-631.

addition, donors like to know about the size and impact of the organization, staff functions, and who other donors are.[10]

Being strategic in investor relations may also mean dealing with a variety of issues that come up in this area of practice. These may include:

- IPO, or initial public offering. This is when a private company decides to "go public" and offer stock for the first time. The SEC has specific guidelines for how this transition must be communicated.

- Stock split, buy-back or other stock quantity changes. A stock split is when a the number of stocks outstanding is split and the price per stock adjusted, with the total value of stocks remaining the same. For example, if you own 100 shares of a stock valued at $200 per share for a total value of $20,000 and the stock splits, you would own 50 shares of the stock valued at $400 per share for a constant $20,000 total value.

- Short selling is when an investor borrows a stock now with a contract to actually buy it later, hoping for a lower price so they profit in the exchange. This is a bad sign because people are anticipating stock price declining.

- M&A. Mergers and acquisitions affect the stock when two companies merge and two stocks become one, and the companies have to determine who the new management will be. The key is to communicate clearly to investors what to expect.

- New product/service announcements, which obviously affect stock price and sales.

- Required reports from SEC. 8K (material changes). 10K (annual report) etc.

- Contentious stockholder meetings, and proxy battles. Since investors are each owners to a degree depending on the number of stocks they own, they must be treated carefully and relationships managed with respect.

---

[10] Penning, T. "(2017) Nonprofit Financial Communications: Donors' Preferred Information Types, Qualities, and Sources. In Laskin, A. (Ed.) Handbook of Investor Relations and Financial Communications. Wiley: Hoboken, NJ.

Tactics

A screen shot of the investor relations page on the Kellogg's website. Notice the various tools for the investor webcast, and also the tabs for financials, governance, and stock information.

There are some unique tactics when it comes to investor relations. Some are applied uniquely to investor relations and some are exclusive to this form of PR practice:

- Annual report. The Securities and Exchange Commission (SEC) requires an annual report of all public companies. In SEC language this is called a 10K and is a form with specific categories of information that must be addressed. However, many companies also enhance and expand on that with a creative and colorful depiction of information for the past year.

- Earnings release and other forms of investor relations news releases. These releases include a stock symbol and often have disclaimer information to state that information in the news release is not "forward looking" prediction of future performance of the stock.

- Various SEC documents beyond annual report and earnings releases that are required.

- Conference calls—these are telephone or online calls with a CEO, CFO and other company representatives and key investors and analysts who can ask financial related questions. These are with a small but important group and a vital way to express information about a company that could persuade investors.

- Annual meetings—investors can attend these in person and vote their shares on key company matters—often just to approve officers terms and compensation, an auditing firm—but can include more significant proposals about company governance. Many investors vote their "proxy" (i.e. not in person at the meeting) via the internet.

- Roadshows—this is like a conference call but where the company executives travel around the country and meet key journalists and analysts in person for meetings and interviews.

- IR page on company web site—it is good practice to have a special link on a company website specifically for investing related information, since investor publics are so important and often demand specific information.

- Social media—the SEC now allows for financial disclosure of "material" (ie relevant to making a stock buying or selling decision) on social media, so long as it is simultaneously shared on other channels and tactics as well.

A final note on tactics is that the regulations of the SEC are stringent to prevent "insider trading," or the situation where someone knows and can act on stock trading information before anyone else and have an unfair advantage. Learn more about finding and distributing stock market information about companies via EDGAR, the SECs online portal.

Evaluation

Evaluation of investor relations can be about the quality of relationships with key investor publics on both the buy side and sell side, and also about the stock price and volume of shares. Generally speaking, evaluation of investor relations includes:

- Analyst reports and their content and positive/negative sentiment;

- Business media coverage of stock, earnings, other aspects of company;

- Purchase of stock

- Stock price

- Volume of stock sold;

- Investor sentiment;

- Number of institutional and individual investors who own stock.

CHAPTER 8: CONSUMER RELATIONS

Consumer relations is the area of public relations that most overlaps with marketing. Marketing and public relations are often confused and the terms can be used interchangeably. It is certainly wrong to say that public relations is a marketing discipline or is somehow underneath marketing. What's worse is to see public relations as merely news releases to assist in the marketing of a product—PR is obviously more than a tactic. In fact, the two fields are parallel and have different areas of emphasis and philosophies.

The root of marketing is "market," and a market is a forum for financial exchange, in other words money is given in exchange for products or services. The essence of public

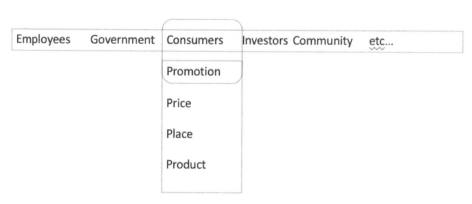

relations is relationships with publics, and the basis of that relationship may or may not be financial in nature as has been shown already in this book.

There certainly is a lot involved with marketing before a financial exchange is made. For years marketers have spoken of the four Ps of marketing—product, price, place, promotion. Product includes identifying a need and designing and developing a product. Place means the channels of distribution and point of purchase strategies. Price involves strategies about pricing for value or prestige or competitiveness in the market. Promotion is where marketing and public relations intersect because it involves the communication aspect of bring a product or service to market.

Public relations sees consumers, the public of focus in marketing, as just one of many publics. And it sees the objective as sales, but more than that. It is about relationships, and out of that sales may be more possible. The chart illustrates the difference between marketing and public relations. Marketing goes deep with regard to consumers, but is focused on one public and sales. PR is broad in terms of its public and objectives for them.

Just as donors were a nonprofit form of investors in the previous chapter, they are the nonprofit version of consumers in this chapter. Consumers, in buying products or services, as the revenue stream for business. Donors, in making contributions, are the revenue source for nonprofits. Some nonprofit also have a form of actual customer, such as those that sell something as a form of fundraising. For example, Habit for Humanity has its Restore where they sell donated used household tools and appliances, using the proceeds for their mission.

There are some public relations trends in recent years with both consumers and donors. With consumers, more and more companies have engaged in relationship marketing, permission marketing and social branding. Relationship and permission marketing means using data and personal knowledge to get to know each consumer's preferences and tailoring efforts to meet them versus broad appeals, and permission means making sure consumers opt-in to share such information and be contacted with this sort of precision. Social branding means that companies care as much how they are known for the activity on social issues and causes as they do for their products and services.

A primary donor trend has been donor intent, meaning if a donor gives money for a specific cause or project, it must be used for its intended use and not redirected to the general budget or some other purpose. Donor activism and donor advised funds reflect that fact that donors want more say in how a nonprofit is run and what it does.

Research

Consumer research is a specialized brand of research. It can include studies of consumer behavior, which includes when people buy things, types of things they are buying, price points that seem most effective and more.

The <u>consumer sentiment index</u> is a measure of how confident consumers are in the economy and an indicator of whether they will be buying in the next months. Consumer confidence studies are similar and good sources of secondary research.

Market research is a more specific form of research. It explores if there is a market for a product or service, and also the characteristics of that market. This includes demographics, geographic areas for the market, the degree of competition in a market and likely market share available for a specific company.

Other research may involve branding research. This would be an assessment of brand preference, or the popularity of one brand of a specific product compared to others. Brand loyalty is a measure of the likelihood of a consumer to be a repeat customer and buy the same brand again when they need to refill or replace a product.

Focus groups and surveys are common methods of research with consumers. Almost every time someone makes a purchase or receives customer service there is a request to complete a satisfaction survey. This is consumer relations research in action.

Objectives

The objectives for consumer relations flow from the research mentioned above, which establishes benchmarks for subsequent evaluation. Each of these can be written with a specific consumer public, often by demographic or psychographic characteristic, and quantified as a number or percentage who say or do a certain desired outcome.

- Brand recognition and preference. Brand recognition is basically an awareness objective, and preference is a form of attitude.

- Social brand objectives measure whether a company's social responsibility efforts are known and valued.

- Repeat customers is a key metric in consumer relations because it shows loyalty. An initial customer deciding to come back is a good sign. In business a related term is "same store sales," which means sales after the first year, because when something is new a lot of people will check it out, but if they come in year two and beyond they must like the product.

- Brand ambassadors and social sharing are more contemporary measures of consumer sentiment, but also the degree to which they promote a company and its products to others. This is typical done on social media and blogs and can be set as an objective in terms of number of posts or the reach of them, or both.

- Sales of course are the obvious and most important action objective. But it is also important to include repeat sales and same-store sales as mentioned above.

- Positive word of mouth and referrals are an objective to get customers or influencers or employees to speak well of a company and its products and refer new customers. Sometimes these referrals are specifically incentivized.

- Positive product reviews in conventional news media and social media.

Strategies

When thinking about strategies in consumer relations it is important to understand the role of PR in consumer relations. There is of course the role of product (or service) publicity. This includes making consumers aware of the product or service, showing the benefits of it to build positive attitude about it, encouraging purchase, and reinforcing satisfaction after purchase.

But there are also advanced roles for PR that can be seen also as strategies. One is customer service that is proactive to ensure positive word of mouth, brand ambassadors and repeat sales. PR people should pay attention to quality management, because a product of poor quality ultimately becomes a consumer relationship issue.

Branding and social branding of the company are a PR role as well. People have relationships with brands, not products or services. Also, many consumers make purchase decisions not only on features and benefits of products, but on the character of a company. How to position a company compared to competitors—i.e. prestige and quality or family-oriented and affordable—is a strategy that PR can carry out. Consumer engagement too, via social media and other channels, is the PR function of building and maintaining relationships with consumers to create an environment in which sales are more likely.

Speaking of branding, while many speak of brand image, it is important to stress reputation more. That is because it is possible for an image to be dishonest and manipulated. An image is just an idea, a mental concept and it can be created in abstraction. A reputation by comparison is based on actual experience and has to be earned. The consumer's actual, real experience determines the company reputation in their mind and not any creative messaging.

The use of influencers has been a popular strategy in recent years. Influencers are the social media version of the older concept of opinion leaders. People become aware of, develop their attitudes about, and decide to purchase products largely by the influence of popular celebrities or knowledgeable individuals. Note that there are some legal concerns here—an influencer must actually have used the product and their communication about it must be from them and not implied. Also, it must be disclosed if influencers are paid to endorse a product or service, since knowing that may determine whether consumers take the recommendation seriously or not.

PR professionals working in consumer relations may be called on to respond to issues as well, such as a product recall, a boycott, or activist consumer groups upset about the way a company produces a product, treats its employees or other company behaviors. The rule of thumb in these cases is to honor the experience and perspective of consumers as much as is appropriate and reasonable. More will be discussed in the chapter on crisis communications.

Corporate social responsibility (CSR), sustainability, and corporate "purpose" as mentioned previously are also a strategic consideration. It used to be these practices gave a company an edge if it wished to push it. But now, these sorts of corporate practices are expected and ignored at the peril of any given company. In fact, a growing trend has been for more companies to become a certified 'B Corporation" to demonstrate to consumers they are worth doing business with. Examples of corporate social responsibility can be found on CSRWire.

Related to CSR is the concept of cause-related marketing. Social responsibility means a company conducts itself not just to earn a profit but also to respect and promote diversity, preserve the environment and contribute in a positive way to society at large. Cause-related marketing means a company partners with a non-profit and/or associates itself with a cause. This assists the marketing to a degree by gaining attention and possibly a product preference because consumers want to help the cause, and it of course helps the non-profit as well. An example is the effort by Gillette, a product for men, to take on the cause of men behaving well toward women, being good fathers and generally aspiring to better behavior.

Tactics

The tactics in consumer behavior can be any of the tactics used in the PESO model mentioned in chapter 3. Ads and social media may predominate, but digital and social media tactics, publicity, brochures, sponsorships and promotional events are also common.

Evaluation

The most important consumer relations evaluation has to do with sales. But there are many other things that could be measured to assure a consumer relations campaign is effective:

- Brand recognition and preference;

- Social brand recognition and favorability;

- Repeat customers, same store sales;

- Brand ambassadors, social sharing, word of mouth and referrals;

- Positive product reviews in the news media

- Social media influencer posts and the engagement that results from them;

All of the above can be measured by a company by looking at its own data and doing surveys and focus groups. In addition, the <u>American Customer Satisfaction Index</u> is a third-party form

of secondary research that can be used for consumer relations evaluation as well on a company or product.

CHAPTER 9: INTERNATIONAL PUBLIC RELATIONS

The publics of international relations are large scale versions of previous publics in this book, but from other countries. For example, the publics of any organization operating in multiple countries could include employees, customers, investors, communities and so on.

This only makes sense when looking at the definition of international public relations:

> *The planned and organized effort of a company, organization, or government to establish mutually beneficial relationships with publics of another nation.*

All three sectors of society participate in international public relations. *Governments* engage in diplomacy and other forms of public relations to promote favorable trade and tourism in their own country. Multi-national corporations (*MNCs*) have offices and factories in more than one country. Nonprofits are known in an international context as non-governmental organizations (*NGOs*) and engage in their mission across many. borders.

In addition to the usual variety of potential publics, there are several that are unique to international PR. One is the governments and government offices and agencies of foreign countries. They can determine whether or not and how an organization from another country can operate within their own borders, and relationships are key. Another form of public is the international media. There are unique characteristics in other countries when it comes to news media as well as advertising outlets, practices, and regulations.

Research

Research in international public relations is especially important. In addition to any of the forms of research mentioned in previous chapters, depending on the campaign or project at hand there will also be other specific forms of research necessary.

One is to know the characteristics of the public in that particular country. Whether employees, customers, investors or community residents, the people of China are no doubt different than the people of the United States. There is also variety within other countries, especially large ones. Some of the key things to know is language and literacy, preferred forms of communication, and key cultural factors (discussed later in this chapter) that may affect whether people will understand and appreciate potential messages.

The government and its laws, especially with regard to media relations and advertising and communication, must be understood before launching a campaign in a foreign country. Some governments have specific restrictions on certain industries based on products, or they restrict how a company can communicate or even limit advertising.

Finally, research on the media, its level of freedom and opportunities must be examined. It is impossible to plan strategy for a PR campaign if unaware of the limitations or unique opportunities to communicate in a particular country.

The U.S. State Department has a wealth of information on other countries that are a good starting point to research other countries, as is the CIA World Fact Book and CountryReports.org . But nothing beats on the ground research in the country with and by residents of the country to have a deep understanding of a country's culture, which can be accomplished with staff or local partners who can conduct primary research or counsel.

Objectives

Objectives internationally will vary based on the nature of the PR campaign. For example, employee relations or consumer relations objectives from previous chapters make sense but would be adapted to the international context. In addition, there are some general objectives associated with conducting PR in other countries:

• Market expansion—many companies set up offices and stores in other countries to expand their market, which means to reach a larger number of customers. So an American company that decides to do business in Germany is expanding its market.

- Acceptance—companies and nonprofits, as well as governments, may face opposition simply because they are foreign. They may also be highly admired for the same reason. But the objective, often before any other work is done, is to gain acceptance by the government, the business community, the media, and citizens at large in a country.

- Recognition—it is also possible that an organization is not even known at all, or not known for its national origin. Being recognized and known as opposed to "flying below radar" is a preliminary objective as well.

- Mutual understanding—in an international context, there will be differences in language, culture, laws and more. Those differences will remain, so the objective is not to change others but to achieve mutual understanding in spite of differences.

Strategies

Strategy specifically applied to an international context is largely related to culture. And there are three things to keep in mind about culture. One, culture is shared by all members of a group, organization or country (albeit with sub-cultures some times). Secondly, culture is passed on subtly from one generation to the next through observed behavior, stories, systems that express what is valued or not. Finally, this culture shapes norms (instinctive ways of doing things) as well as worldview (attitude, the way things are seen). Ignoring culture in international PR is a guarantee of failure.

But how does one understand culture, especially on a global scale? It seems so overwhelmingly complicated. That's what researcher and now consultant Geert Hofstede thought when he developed his "dimensions of culture." These are six dimensions, or scales, that are typical ways cultures vary. It is helpful to consider an organization's host culture and where it is on each scale, and compare it to the cultures around the world where it plans to operate. Knowing the differences can help in strategy planning so an approach is not offensive or ineffective. Here are the dimensions with definitions briefly:

Collectivism – Individualism World map

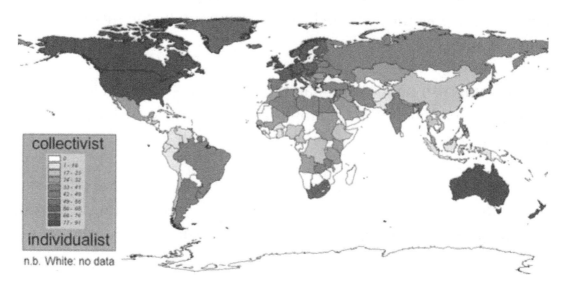

One of Hofstede's culture dimensions and how countries around the world score. From www.geerthofstede.com

- Collectivism-Individualism—in collectivist cultures, people value the group and feel dependent on each other, whereas in individualist cultures people feel more inclined and able to act on their own.

- Power Distance—societies with high power distance accept that there are elites with more power than others, whereas a low power distance reflects a society with egalitarian values of more distributed power and opportunity.

- Masculinity-Femininity—a masculine culture endorses the use of force and competition in society, whereas a feminine culture is less competitive and more nurturing.

- Uncertainty Avoidance—some societies are more tolerant than others of ambiguity and uncertainty. Some cultures prefer obvious clarity.

- Long- vs Short-Term Orientation—long-term cultures are conscious of constant change and prepare for a new future, whereas short-term cultures believe the world changes little and adhering to the past is a good moral compass.

- Indulgent vs Restrained—indulgent cultures believe individuals should be free to pursue their impulses, whereas more restrained cultures value duty to others vs personal satisfaction.

Other cultural variables uncovered by researches include the concept of high or low context. High context cultures derive much meaning from the environment in which communication happens, whereas low context cultures derive meaning primarily from the words. In addition, nonverbal communication varies by culture, including everything from how close one can be to another to gestures and eye gaze. Finally, some societies value task (doing), whereas others value relationships more. Paying attention to these cultural variables can lead to strategy in terms of messages, which media are used, persuasive appeals and more.

Standardize or Specialize?

A large decision that must be made in an international PR effort that involves multiple countries is whether to standardize or specialize. To standardize means to have a global campaign in which the campaign looks largely the same all over the world, with the obvious changes in language. A specialized or international campaign means it is changed to fit the unique cultural aspects of each county. Brand names, product descriptions, slogans and more can vary in an international campaign. Obviously, a standardized campaign is more efficient and good to maintain a global brand. But a specialized campaign can be more effective in each country or market because the target publics will see it as more relevant to them.

The decision to either standardize or specialize a campaign can also be made by considering various factors in the target countries. For example, how similar are the publics across borders, what is the product and its characteristics? Meanwhile, how restrictive are each government, and are the cultural differences significant? The following chart illustrates factors conducive to standardized campaigns and those that would indicate specialization makes more sense. The chart on the next page spells out when to standardize and when to specialize by these factors..

Standardize messages (global)	Specialize messages (international)
Similar target publics	Government is restrictive
Image/visual communication effective and consistently understood	Language differences too great
Appeal to high income/education vs. national identity	Unique cultural differences and preferences
High tech	Economic cycles and seasons vary
Nationalistic characteristics are exportable (eg. Swiss watch, German car)	Country of origin effect is negative
Pan-regional media (same brand and product)	Market by market approach (adapt brand and product)

Meanwhile, Juan-Carlos Mollerda and his research partners came up with a decision-making model to help decide between standardizing and specializing international PR campaigns. Its five steps include considering the necessity to localize, the ability to localize, how much to localize, which tactics to localize, and the metrics to evaluate local effectiveness.

342   J.-C. Molleda et al. / Public Relations Review 41 (2015) 335–344

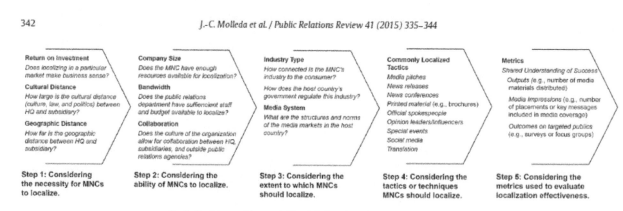

Fig. 1. Decision-making model for global public relations localization efforts.

Another issue that could be a concern or an asset is the "country of origin effect." This is when a company, nonprofit, brand or service is associated highly with a country. This association can be either positive or negative and can change over time. For example, French wine or Japanese autos. If the associated country is admired it would be strategic to play up the country in communications. Otherwise, focusing on the localized brand of a product or the activity of a company within a specific country would be the best approach.

Tactics

While all tactics may apply in an international campaign, language and cultural differences will affect how they are produced. Another option is the use of pan-regional media. That means media outlets in one language that are distributed in print or broadcast in several countries. It is a way to reach large areas of the world efficiently, such as much of Asia or Africa as opposed to just one country. Often, the publics of interest have more in common in terms of income or values than the particular country in which they live.

Evaluation

Evaluation of international PR is two-fold. One is all the usual evaluation methods to see if the typical objectives—changes in target publics awareness, attitude and actions—have been achieved. A second type of international PR evaluation has to do with the MNC or NGOs acceptance, recognition and ability to operate in a country.

Sometimes this evaluation is based on typical methods and metrics that can be quantified to show awareness levels, positive attitudes and specific activities. But it can also be qualitative in nature, such as a letter from a single government official welcoming a company or granting a permit to develop an office in their country.

Part III: Special Situations

This chapter will address two specific situations related to public relations management—crisis communications and integrated communications. These are more about forms of practice than specific publics, so the chapters will not follow the research, objectives, strategies, tactics and evaluation process.

CHAPTER 10: CRISIS COMMUNICATION

Every organization can potentially face a crisis. To some degree, good PR can prevent the type of crisis that comes from unethical behavior, inappropriate behavior and other management error. However, accidents, weather, unreasonable publics and other situations can cause what is considered an organizational crisis.

So what is a crisis? It helps to have a working definition to be able to effectively prevent, respond, and recover from crises. One definition from the Institute for Crisis Management is:

> *Any issue, problem or disruption which triggers negative stakeholder reactions that can impact the organization's reputation, business and financial strength. Crises can be situations threatening or doing harm to people and property, serious disruptions to operations, product recalls, labor issues, social media attacks, lawsuits, highly negative media coverage or allegations of wrongdoing against employees or leaders.*

Put simply, a crisis can affect an organization's operations and/or reputation. Both are key to preserve by preventing a crisis, and, if necessary restore after a crisis. This chapter will therefore look at crisis communications from a proactive and reactive perspective.

Proactive Crisis Communications—Issues Management

The first step in preventing crisis is to know what constitutes a crisis for a particular organization. A crisis at a university may be different than one for a hospital. A crisis for a manufacturing plant would have specific differences than one for the office of a nonprofit organization.

Secondly, before even beginning to think about a specific crisis, an organization should establish its own strategic and ethical philosophy about how to handle crises should they occur. The scholar James Grunig[11] offers four crisis communications principles that serve as guides:

---

[11] Paine. K. (2002). *How to measure your results in a crisis. Institute for Public Relations.* *www.instituteforpr.com*

1. *The Relationship Principle*—an organization can withstand crises better if they have established positive, long-term relationships with publics who may be affected by its decisions

2. *The Accountability Principle*—An organization should take responsibility for crises even when not to blame

3. *The Disclosure Principle*—At a time of crisis, an organization must share what it knows about the crisis and its causes as soon as it knows.

4. *The Symmetrical Communication Principle*—At a time of crisis, an organization must consider the public interest to be at least as important as its own.

These four principles, if put into practice, will help organizations get through and recover from a crisis better than the less wise instincts to lie, deflect, or hide in a crisis.

The question becomes, how does a PR professional prevent crises or be able to identify them soon enough to mitigate them? It may sound simple, but the best advice is to be informed on all aspects of the business, industry and even social trends. Stay current with reading the news media and trade publications, monitor public sentiment on social media and through other opportunities for publics to give feedback. It is wise to initiate dialog, or generally to practice two-way symmetrical communications.

Maintaining mutually beneficial relationships with all publics allows potential crises to bubble up before they blow up. That's why it is good practice to identify and address all "smoldering" issues before they become a crisis, using SWOT (Strengths, Weaknesses, Opportunities, Threats) analysis, environmental scans, crisis plotting grids, and more.

Issues that are not quite yet crises are called para-crises by researchers[12]. The types of para-crises have been organized into clusters:

---

[12] *Coombs, T. & Holladay, S. (2012). The paracrisis: The challenges created by publicly managing crisis prevention. Public Relations Review (38), 3, pp 408-415.*

- Faux pas—an organization had good intentions, but what they did or said was perceived by publics as offensive or insensitive;

- Challenge—an organization's existing practice is accused of being unethical or irresponsible;

- Guilt by association—the organization is associated with a negatively viewed person or another organization;

- Misinformation—information that lacks factual accuracy is circulated about the organization;

- Social media misuse—inappropriate use of what is perceived to be the 'rules' of social media;

- Social media account hack—an organization's social media accounts are hacked and used in a controversial way.

Even though para-crises are not full crises, they still require a response to prevent the situation from getting worse. It's the old idea of "nipping it in the bud" or "getting in front of it." The responses to para-crises have also been categorized. Which one is used depends on the type or cluster the para-crisis falls into and the other aspects of the situation. Response should always be based on the truth of the situation, ethical practice, and the organization's philosophy as discussed above.

Response Strategy	Description
Refusal	Ignore a para-crisis by not responding
Refutation	Deny an accusation and/or attack the accuser *(best to assert correct info and not just deny)*
Repression	Attempts to silence discontented stakeholders (ie remove negative social media posts)
Recognition	Acknowledge validity of negative accusation
Revision	Take action to make changes regarding a faux pas or challenged practice
Refer to Org Values	Refer to values and long-term commitment to address accusation of negative intent
Disassociation	Deny connection with negatively perceived person or organization

Some questions could be asked when deciding if and how to respond to a para-crisis. They include whether publics who matter to the organization expect a response now, whether silence will be seen as indifference or admission of guilt, if others are speaking about the organization and shaping perception, or if waiting will mean losing the ability to affect the outcome

A final aspect of proactive issues management is to prioritize which issues or para-crises should be addressed, or which should receive top priority to handle first. A helpful method to do so is the crisis plotting grid. It has professionals consider how likely something is to happen, and if it happens how much impact would it have on the organization. If both are low there may be no need to act. But if one or both is high it would be worth acting soon to prevent a crisis.

Crisis Plotting Grid

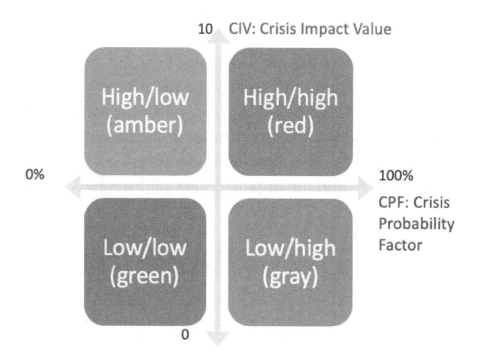

Reactive Crisis Communications—Crisis Plans

If a crisis does happen, then a crisis communications response is necessary. The best thing to have in this case is a crisis communication plan. Such a plan includes the organization's definition of a "crisis" or types of crises so that everyone is on the same page. It should also include the crisis management philosophy and goals for crisis response as discussed above. From a management perspective, the reporting structure and crisis response team members and contact information should be in the plan for easy access, as should media and other contact numbers such as local emergency response departments.

Finally, a crisis plan should have documents prepared in advance to facilitate rapid response. These can include fact sheets, backgrounders, position papers, speaking points on potential issues and more. Each might need to be edited to the specific date and situation but it is better to have anticipated responses written than have to create them from scratch in an emergency. In addition, forms to document calls received, actions taken and other processes are helpful to have ready to easily fill out details for subsequent analysis of the crisis response once the situation cools down.

In crisis communications, the process is generally as follows:

1. Assess type and nature of crisis, level of risk.

2. Adapt the crisis plan to specific crisis at hand.

3. Respond—execute the crisis communication plan.

4. Recovery—ongoing communication even when attention has waned.

5. Review and adjust plan for next crisis.

Crisis Response Theories and Strategies

Crisis communications has been well studied and written about by scholars and professionals alike. What follows are three crisis communication theories and a collection of practical response strategies as well. First is the Contingency Theory[13], which essentially says that the response is contingent on the nature of the crisis. The theory places a range of potential responses on a scale between two extremes— pure advocacy on one end and pure accommodation on the other. Advocacy

---

[13] *Pang, Augustine; Ji, Yan; and Cameron, Glen T.. Contingency theory of strategic conflict management: Unearthing factors that influence ethical elocution in crisis communication. (2010). 13th International Public Relations Research Conference: Coral Gables, Florida, March 10-13 2010*

means the organization fights to get its own way and win the argument in the crisis, whereas accommodation involves giving in to the opposing parties. Again, responses anywhere on the continuum may be deployed depending on the nature of the crisis and the organization's culture, ethics, management perspective, and public relations training of the professionals in charge of the response.

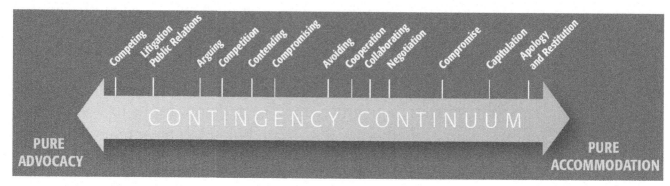

Contingency Theory

A second and related theory is William Benoit's Image Restoration Theory. It focuses more, as the name implies, not just on the response but on the objective to restore an organization's image (recall the preference stated earlier in this book for reputation as opposed to image). Here are the basic response types identified by Benoit for organizations seeking to restore their image after a crisis, starting with the most defensive and moving to more bending to the public sentiment:

• Denial

• Evade Responsibility
  • *Scapegoat; claim it was an accident; not feasible to prevent*

• Reduce Offensiveness
  • *Bolster affection toward organization; attack the accuser; offer compensation; minimize the severity of the situation*

• Corrective action
  • *Fix the problem, commit to change*

• Mortification
  • *Apologize, admit fault*

The third crisis communications theory is the most famous: Situational Crisis Communication Theory (SCCT), first proposed by Timothy Coombs and since studied by many other scholars and adapted by many professionals. The theory is based on years of observations of actual crises and responses, and identified three types of crises or clusters into which they all fit—*preventable, accident, or victim*. If a crisis is the result of an accident or an organization is the victim of a crisis, they are less likely to be blamed or suffer reputational damage. If however a crisis was preventable, and the organization bears responsibility and their response should reflect that.

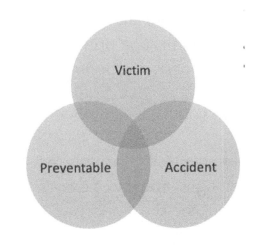

SCCT also identifies a set of response types, similar to those in the first two theories. Which response is chosen again depends on the type of crisis, as well as organizational factors. For example, if an organization is a victim, an attack the accuser response, as harsh as it sounds, may be appropriate. But if the crisis was preventable, an apology may be the most ethical and effective response. Here are the SCCT response types:

- Attack the accuser

- Denial of the crisis or the organization's part in it

- Scapegoat, placing blame on others

- Excuse, claim the situation was beyond organizational control

- Justification, acknowledge organizational role in crisis but claim actions or statements were necessary

- Compensation, provide monetary assistance or other means to alleviate harm done to others

- Apology, admit fault and intent to change

In addition to these theoretical descriptions of types of crises and related responses, there are a variety of specific strategies for responding to crises. These are communication principles that describe what is said and done within a categorical crisis response:

- Prove you have identified situation and are DOING something;

- Share news of crisis quickly; shift story to be about your response. This is called "getting in front of" a crisis because the first to respond usually frames and defines the situation;

- Maintain communication so you are the source for the story;

- Communicate only the facts; not speculation;

- Be decisive and confident when you speak;

- Have a single spokesperson related to the crisis.

When making a statement in response to a crisis, specific words will vary of course. But a recommended structure for a statement in terms of what to include in what order is as follows:

- Acknowledge….facts of event/issue

- Empathy…if there are victims

- Values…frame response in terms of org values (intent)

- Approach….how and what you'll DO

- Commitment….establish organizational role going forward

Evaluating Crisis Response

A lot of organizations may be tempted to breathe a sigh of relief when a crisis appears to be over and the spotlight is off. But from a PR management perspective it is more important to know how the organization handled the crisis. Also, it is dangerous to assume that just because a crisis is not getting a lot of attention in the media or among certain publics that the problem is over. People remember, and could be silently bearing resentment and speaking negatively about an organization because of their perception and experience in the crisis. Therefore, reputation of an organization should be measured during, at the immediate end, and months after the crisis.

In brief, here is what to measure to assess the crisis communication effectiveness:

- Output—are messages getting out and to whom?

- Impact—is public opinion being affected in short term?

- Outcome—long-term, have your key relationships been restored so that crisis does not hurt sales, donations, employee retention, investor confidence and other reputational and relational measures with key publics?

A final word on crisis communications: your reactions to the situations in life are more important than the situations themselves. People will much more remember how an organization responds to a crisis than they will the crisis itself. In this respect, a crisis for an ethical and well-trained PR professional is not only a problem, it could well be an opportunity to gain in reputation by demonstrating competence and character.

CHAPTER 11: INTEGRATED COMMUNICATIONS

This final chapter is brief, but important. At stake is how the very nature of public relations is defined, understood and appreciated by others in management positions.

The key here is to bring back what was stressed in the first chapter. Public relations is a *management* function. It is not, repeat NOT, a tactic in service to other fields.

The problem is that people in other management positions, be they finance, management, human resources, or marketing, consider "PR" to be a synonym for publicity or media relations. The field started that way in the early 1900s with "press agents," but quickly became a more sophisticated profession concerned with multiple tactics and the overall objective of helping organizations achieve their mission through facilitating productive relationships with various publics. Recall Arthur Page and the Page Principles from chapter 1.

This is all raised here because of the popular concept of Integrated Marketing Communications, or IMC. Notice the title of this chapter is Integrated Communications, leaving out the word marketing. That is by design.

IMC emerged because the functions of advertising, marketing, and public relations were not coordinated or conducted in a unified strategy. Hence the term integrated. The problem with saying integrated "marketing" communications is that it only integrates things for the purposes of marketing, or consumer relations. Therefore, integrated communications is a better term because it speaks to the need for a unified strategy when communicating with all the publics addressed in each chapter of this book.

Nevertheless, some coined the term IMC to mean:

• Messages that address multiple consumer and non-consumer audiences and achieve synergy of messages and timing

• Strategic coordination of multiple communication voices

• Coordination of advertising, public relations and marketing

The 4As (the American Association of Advertising Agencies) defined IMC this way:

> *Marketing communications planning that recognizes the added value of a comprehensive plan that evaluates the strategic value of a variety of communication disciplines and combines those disciplines to promote clarity, consistency, and maximum communications impact.*

That definition's mention of a "variety of communications disciplines" is speaking about the fact that advertising, public relations, and marketing often worked in "silos" (as seen in farm photo at right), which means they never interacted, planned together or were integrated in their approach. That makes sense, but the problem is in how the three disciplines were defined:

• Marketing= promoting and distributing a product/service to customers

• Advertising = use of controlled media to influence a target audience

• Public relations = use of earned media to raise awareness and influence target publics

Each of these are not wrong exactly; they are just not complete. In the case of public relations, it limits and dumbs down the profession to merely "earned media," or a tactic. As has been demonstrated in this book, public relations can deploy any tactic you can think of, all of the types of tactics in the PESO model.

No, PR is about relationships. It is about fulfilling organizational objectives. It is a **management function.**

IC vs. IMC

This is why many scholars and public relations professionals prefer the term Integrated Communication (IC), which is broader, does not define PR as a marketing tool, and is more beneficial to organizations.

IMC integrates *marketing* communications, primarily targeting *customers* and potential customers, for the single objective of *sales*. In this respect IMC is merely tactical.

IC integrates all communications from all functions of an organization—including marketing, finance, human resources and more—to fulfill multiple objectives as spelled out in all the chapters of this book. Therefore, IC is more strategic, philosophical, and management oriented.

Another way to think about it is what is integrated? In IMC, tactics and strategies are integrated. But if you think about it, what is an ad, a brochure, a web site? Is it marketing or advertising or public relations? Most people could not say. That's because the disciplines are not tactics and should not be defined as such. These days, any tactic could be used in any of these disciplines.

No, what really is integrated in IC is the publics and the objectives. In any campaign, any public could see it. A consumer campaign could be seen by investors or employees. A public affairs campaign could be seen by the community. Therefore, IC helps to maintain message consistency.

Tom Harris of Northwestern University has offered this useful definition of IC:

> *IC uses an appropriate combination of sending, receiving and interactive tools drawn from a wide range of communication disciplines to create and maintain mutually beneficial relationships between an organization and key stakeholders, including customers.[14]*

---

[14] Harris, T. *Value Added Public Relations; The Secret Weapon of Integrated Marketing.* (1999). McGraw-Hill.

Notice how this definition doesn't define disciplines as tools but acknowledges they each have tools. Also, the focus is on mutually beneficial relationships between an organization and key stakeholders—the very definition of public relations in the first place. Harris tags on "including customers" just to stress that they are not the only public of interest.

A final thought on integration is to think about the levels of integration. Organizations can only do so tentatively and integrate how they present themselves to the outside world (image), or they can adopt more thorough integration of communication throughout the organization. That is the essence of PR as a management function. Here are the levels of integration from least to most:

• Image = consistent look and feel (a branding concern);

• Functional = all communications functions are at management level;

• Coordinated = any function, not just marketing, can lead integration;

• Customer-based = outside-in, driven by customer databases;

• Stakeholder-based = driven by needs of ALL publics, not just customers;

• Relationship management = all functions work together at management level with the objective of mutual relationships with all publics.

The bottom line: for a PR person to get a seat at the management table, it is wise to describe the profession as integrated communication.

Made in the USA
Monee, IL
05 August 2023

40487156R00050